The Novels of Wole Soyinka

The Intellectual and Society
in
THE NOVELS OF WOLE SOYINKA

M. RAJESHWAR

PRESTIGE

Published by
Prestige Books
3/28, East Patel Nagar, New Delhi 110 008
in association with
Indian Society for Commonwealth Studies
New Delhi

ISBN: 81-85218-21-8

Jacket design by
3-A Corporation,
New Delhi 110 002

Phototypesetting by
data culture
New Delhi 110 065
Ph. 6431070

Printed at
Mehra Offset Press
New Delhi 110 002

CONTENTS

	Foreword	13
	Preface	17
1.	Introduction: Soyinka's Novels and the African Context	21
2.	An Engagement with Reality: *The Interpreters*	37
3.	Never Too Late to Regain Paradise: *Season of Anomy*	57
4.	Towards a Conclusion: African Reality and Soyinka's Art in Perspective	80
	Bibliography	87
	Index	95

An intellectual is . . . in essence a social critic, a person whose concern is to identify, to analyze, and in this way to help overcome the obstacles barring the way to the attainment of a better, more humane, and more rational social order. As such he becomes the conscience of society and the spokesman of such progressive forces as it contains in any given period of history.

Paul Baran

For Amulya

Acknowledgements

I wish to record my deep sense of gratitude to Prof. P. Mallikarjuna Rao who not only supervised my research work but also taught me the importance of disciplined expression in the writing of my thesis with his scholarly guidance and personal affection.

My profound thanks are due to Prof. S. Laxmana Murthy and Prof. Dinker Srideshmukh but for whose wise counsel, constant help and inspiration it would have been impossible for me to complete my research.

I gratefully acknowledge my indebtedness to Dr A. Jaganmohana Chari, Reader in English, who has patiently gone through the press copy and made some valuable suggestions.

I am deeply indebted to the University Grants Commission, New Delhi for awarding me Junior Research Fellowship with which I met the expenditure involved in my research work.

I am also thankful to the Librarian of the Central Institute of English and Foreign Languages, Hyderabad for permitting me to use the Library for several weeks.

Finally, I owe my sincere thanks to M/s Prestige Books who spared no efforts in bringing out the book neatly and promptly.

M. RAJESHWAR

Foreword

The true test for African literature could lie only in African reality. Therefore, for an evaluation of African literature, we have to approach African history itself. The darkness of the "dark continent" has been turned into an almost metaphysical idea in more than one respect. Anthropology, culture, race, religion, and even literature of the capitalist Europe have condemned Africa to a position of inferiority in the absolute sense.

The European colonizers tried to do the same thing to the peoples of their Asian colonies like India too. But in the case of India, they had to grapple with a more settled and more deeply entrenched class and its civilization. It was almost a herculean task for them to rub in their own epiphenomenological aspects, into the Indian reality, especially in the field of culture. But the European colonizers of Africa succeeded in reducing the consciousness of its peoples into the acceptance of their own being an inferior category which is responsible for the idea of magnitude. This was possible perhaps because in African countries the social formations had not undergone structural changes on class lines before the advent of the colonial rule. But the Western education as usual and as true as in the case of all colonial states has also created a sense of retrospection and introspection among the African intellectuals. The consequent sense of self-knowledge obviously led them to such questions as identification, commitment and freedom in social, political and economic terms. And the result is anti-colonial struggles waged in several African states in this century. However, the African countries which have been politically freed, are yet to attain economic and cultural independence. It is in this context that literature as a part of cultural praxis, wherein the aforementioned struggle is carried on, becomes an important weapon in the hands of African intellectuals like Wole Soyinka, Achebe and Ngùgi.

But where the intellectual effort exists as a phenomenon separate from the economic realities and historical context of the society it tends to become elitist and idealistic—something that can be observed in certain African writers and intellectuals.

Soyinka as a literary artist gives one the impression of being an elitist idealist, at least in the beginning of his career if one follows the argument of Mr. M. Rajeshwar in this book. However, as an African intellectual who is closely involved in the historical predicament of his country, Soyinka envisages his intellectual fictional heroes as undergoing a transition on the same lines as propounded by Frantz Fanon in *The Wretched of the Earth.* This fact is demonstrated sufficiently well by the author. But this transition—from the position of the intellectual's assimilation of the culture of the ruling power, the consequent estrangement from his traditional society leading to his eagerness to identify himself with his own cultural past and finally to the acceptance of his role as an awakener and liberator of his people—turns out to be a fictional mode of realizing the potential of intellectual as liberator. The important question, one is tempted to ask here, is: Has this exercise enabled Soyinka to become a revolutionary in practice or be the guiding force behind one? Soyinka is, no doubt, an artist whose characters are not mere mouthpieces. He has succeeded in the depiction of African reality through his intellectual heroes who have got the anguished revolutionary thrust in them.

His fictional works also abound in technical and aesthetic virtuosity, especially in the employment of Yoruba myths for structural purposes. But the emphasis on the artistic values *vis-a-vis* the politico-social issues only places them as polarities in a position of antithesis. Artistic values are only reflexive of the primary content of politico-social issues. Without thc latter, the former are not only devoid of rationale for their existence but an emphasis on them alone also obscures and mystifies the issues.

Soyinka's literary output is still rich in excellence on account of his basic commitment to African reality, although his bias for artistry has never ceased to be an irritant in its enjoyment. His writings have helped him as a mode of self-clarification. However, their position as part of the African revolutionary cultural praxis needs to be established.

A. Jaganmohana Chari

Department of English
Kakatiya University
Warangal 506 009

Preface

Wole Soyinka's novels are so significant a contribution to the world of the English language novel that they certainly merit a full-length study. But Soyinka as a novelist continues to be neglected by critics at home and abroad. His reputation as a poet and playwright seems to have eclipsed his achievement as a novelist. Significant critical pronouncements on his literary output are invariably based on his poetical and dramatic works only, and are sometimes grossly unsympathetic. A thorough evaluation of his novels is likely to steer him clear of several charges levelled against him, because these novels faithfully portray the almost cathartic experience of Soyinka.

Among the middle-brow critics, he is known as an "anglo-modernist" and his writings as "Euro-assimilationist" literature.[1] Chinweizu, who represents this group, has charged Soyinka with ignoring his responsibility towards his nation by indulging in "Shamanist mystifications" which the lay reader cannot easily decode. In essence the attack on Soyinka focuses on two points: he lacks a concrete social vision that would like to have his works serve extra-literary ends and his "obscurity" that throws into question the relevance of his works to African life.

The high-brow academic critics have, however, put up a spirited defence of Soyinka, especially after the Nobel award. Molara Ogundipe-Leslie while establishing Soyinka's universality defends his special use of the English language which has earned him many adverse comments: "Soyinka's mastery of English is at that high level where expertise breaks the semantic barrier to poetic efflorescence and linguistic newness. At that level of control, one becomes one of the makers of the language." Isidore Ekpewho emphasizes the "essential *mythic* foundations" of Soyinka's art and argues that "Soyinka is perhaps the most truly African writer today because he articulates the African condition through the medium of aesthetic essences derived from the timeless cultural history of his people."

I have given the above account of the critical response to Soyinka's works to underline the fact that his fiction, though impressive, is totally ignored when judging his achievement as a writer. Whatever his detractors and admirers have to say about his African roots or the lack of them and the literary validity of his obscurity or otherwise, his novels give the lie to the whole controversy.

A perceptive reading of his novels proves that his artistic sensibility is indubitably shaped by African history—past and present. In his novels, he not only fictionally relives the African reality but also envisions a better social order expecting the progressive-minded among his countrymen to strive for its realization. The present endeavour is to study Soyinka's fictional heroes in their role as leaders of the struggle against the colonial and neo-colonial forces stubbornly resisting the process of social regeneration in Africa. The final chapter attempts to make a minute and disinterested analysis of various aspects of Soyinka's style and establishes its variety and richness. Ideas appear to come to Soyinka's mind in a rush leaving him little time to organize them in a neat pattern or tune them to a coherent rhythm. To add to this, he religiously upholds artistic values often to the detriment of the uninitiated reader's ready enjoyment of his work.

These and other dimensions of Soyinka's fictional world, discussed at length in this book, are expected to firmly establish Soyinka's place in the realm of the very best of novelists writing in

English.

In writing this book, I have been benefited by the insights of several Soyinkan scholars. Particular mention may be made of Eldred Jones, Gerald Moore and James Booth.

NOTES

1. For a detailed discussion, see Bernth Lindfors, "Beating the White Man at His Own Game: Nigerian Reactions to the Nobel Prize in Literature," *The Literary Criterion,* XXV, 1 (1990), pp. 43-59.

Introduction
Soyinka's Novels and the African Context

I

With the award of the Nobel Prize for Literature to Wole Soyinka in 1986, the seal of international recognition was eventually laid on African Literature. The award jolted the European and American critics from their surprisingly long condescension towards the "new literatures" including the African writing in English. For once they shed their patronizing airs and began to pay serious attention to the Anglophone African writers in general and to Soyinka in particular.

The incorporation of unfamiliar anthropological material, fictionalization of nationalist and political aspirations and the recent trend of treating social and existential problems in artistic terms have lent a complex character to African writing. Soyinka's works being very representative share many of the concerns of the African writers. Any critical study dealing with his novels should of necessity bring to it an historio-social perspective of the whole continent.

Before Africa's interaction with Europe, its numerous races and ethnic groups lived a simple life—in close affinity with nature. They had their rituals and observances which gave meaning to their existence. Every small community had its own world-view which was characterized by intellectual and moral independence. In their narratives, the European adventurers and mariners, who explored Africa in the nineteenth century, had registered great admiration for the age-old African institutions and its self-sufficient societies. In his Nobel address, Soyinka eloquently acknowledges this fact. He says:

> They [the adventurers] spoke of living communities which regulated their own lives, which had evolved a working relationship with Nature, which ministered to their own wants and secured their future with their own genius.[1]

Accounts of these European travellers to Africa deeply disturbed the European savants and philosophers—Hegel, Locke, Montesquieu, Hume and Voltaire, to name a few—who held for ages a poor opinion of Africa and its peoples. Till then they unabashedly believed Africa to be a "dark continent," its people barbarians and its institutions primitive. In spite of ample evidence to the contrary, they doggedly clung to this view of Africa. The European scientists and theorists of human evolution had their share to contribute in this regard. To meet the Africans on a reasonably equal footing and to accord them the recognition as fellow human beings was unacceptable to them. Caught in this irksome situation, the European philosophers were necessitated to denigrate Africa and its way of life. To maintain their racial superiority they took to mystification of the plain truth about Africa and consequently it remained a "dark continent," at least for the outsiders, for many more years.

The European colonizers of Africa were undoubtedly guided by the views of their philosophers. The colonialists were quick to realize that economic plundering of Africa would not last long unless the exploited people were made to feel inferior to themselves. With this aim, they evolved ingenious strategies to instil inferiority complex among the African natives. The independent African societies were strategically dismantled by them. The values these societies cherished since time immemorial were openly and flagrantly denigrated. Soon the cultural and religious institutions of Africa had either totally collapsed or were distorted beyond recognition. African history and culture had been misinterpreted to serve the selfish ends of the colonialists. Frantz Fanon aptly says:

> Colonialism is not satisfied merely with holding a people in its grip and emptying the native's brain of all form and

> content. By a kind of perverted logic it turns to the past of the oppressed people and distorts, disfigures and destroys it.[2]

The ceaseless efforts of the colonialists ultimately destroyed the very African character of these societies. As a part of effecting this miraculous historical change, the colonialists employed such passive methods as conversion of Africans to the Christian Faith and the imposition of the European methods of educating the young.

The European system of education had both positive and negative effects. Under its influence many educated Africans grew to despise their own culture and history and they soon began to look upto the Europeans for intellectual guidance. Chiekh Hamidou Kane aptly sums up the damage caused by the Western education to the African psyche in his *Ambiguous Adventure:* "Better than the cannon, it, the school, makes conquest permanent. The cannon compels the body, the school bewitches the soul."[3] The positive result was that, at a later stage, some of these Western-educated Africans mustered up courage to question the very righteousness of the European domination of Africa. These African intellectuals had sown the first seeds of dissatisfaction with the colonial rule among their people and it is largely due to their efforts that the African nations are at least politically independent today.

Even though the edifice of colonialism was formally dismantled in the early sixties, its evil legacy continues to characterize the social and religious institutions and tenor of life in Africa, more so in Nigeria to which Soyinka belongs. During the colonial rule the peoples across the continent were subjected to ruthless exploitation. As a result, there is a striking similarity in the problems faced by these societies today. Corruption, in all walks of life, has become the order of the day. Chinua Achebe's observation on the situation in the early years of independent Nigeria may be extended to the entire continent in the post-colonial phase:

> Within six years of independence Nigeria was a cesspool of corruption. Public servants helped themselves freely to the nation's wealth. . . . Elections were blatantly rigged. . . . The

> national census was outrageously stage-managed; judges and magistrates were manipulated by politicians in power. The politicians themselves were manipulted and corrupted by foreign business interests.[4]

The democratic rule itself was a short-lived political phenomenon in a majority of African states. Within a few years of independence from the colonial yoke, military coups swept across the continent. The self-serving military dictators callously allowed the Western powers to operate from behind the scenes on the African soil chiefly in the form of multi-national corporations and military assistance. Soyinka, while calling the present-day Africa a monstrous child born to the intellectual dishonesty of the colonialists, says that it "draws material, nourishment, breath and human recognition from the strengths and devices of that world; with an umbilical cord which stretches across oceans."[5] He emphasizes the urgent need to "sever that cord" and urges to "leave this monster of a birth to atrophy and die or to rebuild itself on long-denied humane foundations."[6]

As things stand now, the African societies are caught in a deep identity crisis. A deep chasm divides the traditional African life and the materialistic Western life which the Africans have assimilated. To return to the pre-colonial culture, which the Negritudinists have advocated, would mean going back to the bush-man's life which is well nigh impossible and undesirable in the modern context. On the other hand, to remain in the embrace of the Western culture obviously means to sacrifice the African character of African life. Added to this dilemma are the crises so often created by the neo-colonialist and imperialist forces. Whenever the economic and political interests of these imperialists are in danger, they create conflicts among people and nations. The example which comes immediately to our mind is the Biafran-Nigerian civil war which caused untold misery, suffering and great loss of human life.

Such political, economic and cultural turmoils have made great demands on the African intellectuals, specially the writers. They have been forced to take a definite stand on many issues. The foremost task they have taken on themselves is to interpret the present African reality. The writers, being the conscience of the society, are perhaps the best qualified persons to speak for it. The African writers have realized quite early their crucial role in giving their people a new confidence. Writing has been almost a mission for them. Ever since they started writing, they have been sensitively alive to the political and social changes on the continent. Their themes have shown great variety. In the beginning, their chief concerns were countering the distorted version of the African past and the evil consequences of European hegemony. With the passage of time, their concerns and preoccupations changed and today there is a bewildering variety in their themes.

Notwithstanding the various ideologies the African writers adhere to, every one of them has taken keen interest in and shown great concern for society. They have endeavoured, against heavy odds, to expose corruption and hypocrisy so rampantly prevalent in the contemporary African societies. Achebe's *A Man of the People* and Ayi Kwci Armah's *The Beautiful Ones Are Not Yet Born* are scathing indictments of the corrupt post-colonial African society. Other writers such as Ngugi wa Thiong'o, on account of their leftist sympathies, are not satisfied with the mere exposure of the corrupt society. These writers have written ideologically-coloured novels which sometimes are didactic, to give whatever direction they can, to their aimlessly advancing society.

II

Soyinka, who occupies a prominent place among the African writers, is not explicitly political like Ngugi and others. He is one of those artists who do not subordinate artistic values to political considerations even when he is committed to a political cause. He is very conscious of the important role he can play as an artist in shaping the destiny of his society. The general impression we have from a reading of Soyinka's works is that he has made it his mission to examine the traditional structures of his society with the intention of gleaning whatever is relevant and useful from the African past which he hopes to make use of, in suggesting a future course of action for his society.

Soyinka, who has tried his hand at almost all genres of literature, has written only two novels to date. His accomplishment as a novelist can be fully understood only when we examine these novels against the historical and literary background of Africa as suggested above. Though Soyinka's main literary output is in the field of drama, his two novels are a valuable contribution to African fiction. With the publication of his first novel, *The Interpreters*, in 1965, it was widely believed that a new mode of fiction had arrived on the African literary scene. With its multiple intellectual protagonists and complex plot, *The Interpreters* was markedly different from the African novels that preceded it. As a result, Soyinka has earned the reputation of being a "difficult" novelist. In spite of this complexity and meagre output Soyinka has carved an enviable niche for himself in the realm of African fiction. Kolawole Ogungbesan rightly observes:

> Soyinka as a novelist deserves to be taken seriously because of his high intellectual position among African writers. A speculative thinker, his persistent call to African writers to demonstrate that they have a vision shows that he sees *the literary artist as a redeemer*. He believes that the writer possesses an inner light unavailable to the mass of his people, and that it is his *duty to guide his society* towards a beautiful future.[7] (Emphasis added)

As a part of this onerous task of guiding his society, Soyinka has made a thorough analysis of the Nigerian society and suggested ways to overcome the evils plaguing it. He feels that only intellectuals who form the thinking faculty of the society can match to that stupendous task. This fact goes a long way in explaining his preference for intellectual characters to people his novels. The use of intellectuals as fictional heroes is a fairly recent trend in the Anglophone African novels, if not in the West. We can say, without much hesitation, that, in Africa, this tradition started with the publication of Soyinka's *The Interpreters.* In this novel, as well as in *Season of Anomy,* his second novel, Soyinka has chosen to examine the predicament of the intellectuals in a corrupt society and their contribution to social change.

Soyinka has dealt with intellectual characters in his plays also. But there is a marked difference between his portrayal of intellectuals in his plays and in his fiction. Most of the intellectuals in his plays are either ineffective or degenerate geniuses unlike their counterparts in the novels. In Soyinka's play, *The Lion and the Jewel,* the intellectual, Lakunle, is shown as one who is effeminate with "his head stuffed with bits and pieces of Western culture." *The Road* is a superb accomplishment of Soyinka as a dramatist. Soyinka endeavours to clarify the relationship between the contemporary Nigerian life and Yoruba myth in this play. The chief character is Professor, an ex-Sunday school teacher. He deals in spare-parts retrieved from lorry wrecks on the road. Whether he himself caused these "accidents" by secretly removing the road-signs is a matter of conjecture. Professor is a kind of businessman-cum-prophet. He is loved, admired and held in great awe and reverence by the truck drivers. Professor uses the Yoruba god Ogun, who represents the creative and destructive essence, to stage the enactment of the Resurrection. Soon he is possessed by the pagan god and the madness culminates in a melodramatic death on the stage.

While *The Road* has a perverted intellectual for its main character, the *Madmen and Specialists* has a misguided intellectual for its protagonist. Dr. Bero joins the medical corps during the Nigerian civil war. Once at the war front, he is forcibly drafted into intelligence work and before he can realize what has happened he is already playing with the lives of others. The change in Dr. Bero's profession has a damaging influence on his father who loses his mental poise. Dr. Bero grows power-hungry and he is ready to stoop to any level of dehumanization. At the end, after the nefarious deeds committed without any pricks of conscience, he is back home, happy and healthy. He need do no penance.

The intellectuals we encounter in Soyinka's novels, with very few exceptions, are just the opposite of the ones who appear in his plays. They are all men of principles. They hope to live by an ideology whether self-made or borrowed. Further, they have all been victims of a corrupt establishment which they seek to change for the better.

Before we examine the role the intellectuals play in giving a direction to their society in Soyinka's fiction, it is useful to relate them to Frantz Fanon's perspective on the African intellectuals. The observations which Fanon made in the context of colonial Africa are still relevant as the colonial situation has not substantially altered in Africa even today. Only political power has passed from the European imperialists to black oppressive forces represented by military juntas, corrupt politicians and multi-national corporations. The role of the intellectual in the African society, as defined by Fanon, holds good as long as political suppression and corruption continue.

In the colonial era, Fanon says, the native intellectual "takes up arms to defend his nation's legitimacy and . . . wants to bring proof to bear out that legitimacy."[8] For this purpose, he will be "obliged to dissect the heart of his people."[9] Clearly, Fanon has assigned the African intellectual the role of analyzing and leading his society. His book *The Wretched of the Earth* has studied the participation of the native intellectuals, specially the writers, in social and cultural change in three phases.

In the first phase, which is a period of "unqualified assimilation," the intellectual assimilates the culture of the ruling power and gets estranged from his traditional society. He cuts his last moorings and breaks adrift from his people. But this phase is not to last long. The intellectual is quick to grasp that the alien culture has made him a stranger in his own land. The degradation his people suffer at the hands of the oppressive forces awakens him to a new reality. He begins to have a split personality. He can neither totally embrace the foreign culture nor return to his people because, by this time, he has already lost his roots. It is here that the second phase starts. In this stage the intellectual is thoroughly disturbed. In a desperate attempt to identify himself with his people, he immerses himself in his cultural past. Going down his memory lane, he reinterprets old legends in the light of a "borrowed aestheticism." Achebe's *Things Fall Apart* and *Arrow of God* and Armah's *Two Thousand Seasons* are visionary reconstructions of the past. These novels bear proof of Fanon's dictum about the second stage in the intellectual evolution of the African natives.

The third phase, which follows close on the heels of the second, is characterized by fighting. By this time the writer-intellectual "instead of according the people's lethargy an honoured place in his esteem . . . turns himself into an awakener of the people."[10]

Though Fanon appears to have been dissatisfied with the actual performance of the African intellectuals, he nevertheless expects them to closely align themselves with the people fighting against oppression if the situation so demands and become full-fledged revolutionaries to launch an all-out fight against all forms of oppression, be it colonial, neo-colonial or imperialist. Ngugi too seems to be at one with Fanon's expectations when he vehemently asserts:

> I believe that African intellectuals must align themselves with the struggle of African masses for a meaningful national ideal. For we must strive for a form of social organization that will free the manacled spirit and energy of people so we can build new country, and sing a new song.[11]

Soyinka and his intellectual heroes seem to correspond to Fanon's formulations about African intellectuals. Soyinka studied abroad and suffered alienation from his people to some extent. He dug up the old legends and reinterpreted them in the light of the contemporary realities. For example, his long evocative poem *Idanre* celebrates the creation myth of the Yoruba god, Ogun, who occupies a prominent place in Soyinka's works. Soyinka's harrowing experiences with the oppressive forces after the Nigerian independence made him some kind of a revolutionary. *Season of Anomy* is born out of this phase of Soyinka's intellectual growth.

Like their creator, the young intellectuals of his novels are educated abroad. They come home with very high hopes and colourful dreams of participating in the nation-building work. They enter different fields as professionals and immediately find themselves face to face with the worst form of corruption and hypocrisy in all walks of life such as politics, education and religion. Their individual sensibility, says Ogungbesan, is "at war with the claims of society [but they] are strong enough to contain to a large extent the influence of society upon themselves."[12] *The Interpreters,* the first novel, concludes in the intellectuals becoming wiser, battered and bruised by their experiences, in an essentially corrupt society. The protagonists of *Season of Anomy,* which in more than one sense comes as a sequel to *The Interpreters*, take off where their counterparts in the earlier novel have stopped. They have all the experience of the interpreters. Besides, they are ideologically equipped to lead their society towards an envisioned goal. They take up the cudgels on behalf of the progressive forces of society and are ready to resort even to the use of violence for the actualization of their visions, because on their way they have to encounter regressive and oppressive forces who do not hesitate to nip in the bud anything that threatens their existence. And at the end of the novel, there is evidence to show that the intellectuals are going to succeed in their mission. Thus although it cannot be conclusively established that Soyinka consciously allowed himself to be influenced by Fanon's ideas, the parallels between Fanon's paradigm about the African intellectuals and Soyinka's fictional treatment of them are unmistakable—so unmistakable as the relevance of Freud's concept of Oedipus Complex to D.H. Lawrence's *Sons and Lovers.*

The basic theme in Soyinka's fiction, as it should be obvious by now, is the relation between the intellectual and society and the intellectual's role in the transformation of society. The role which Soyinka envisions for the intellectual is that of a dynamic force. He believes that society has an inherent mechanism which changes it but the person who expedites this change and gives it proper direction is always the intellectual. So he

> sees society as being in continual need for salvation from itself. This act of salvation is not a mass act; it comes about through the vision and dedication of individuals who doggedly pursue their vision in spite of the opposition of the very society they seek to save. They frequently end up as the victims of the society which benefits from their vision.[13]

Soyinka's depiction of this organic and dynamic relation between the intellectual and society will be treated at length in the next few pages. Fanon has been alluded to at relevant places, as his theory about the third-world intellectuals is, as has been stated earlier, quite helpful to this study.

Before we discuss Soyinka's novels elaborately in the light of the aforementioned theme, it is important to take into consideration what a cross-section of critics have said about Soyinka's novels and their themes. Soyinka has engaged substantial critical attention both at home and abroad. But a review of the existing critical scholarship shows that no full-length study has been attempted to discuss Soyinka's social concerns and the theme of the intellectual and society as major factors shaping his fiction.

Juliet Okonkwo, in her perceptive study of the essential unity of the two novels, underlines their common theme as "the intellectual and his responsibility in a new nation."[14] She categorizes the characters of *The Interpreters* as "psycho-passive" intellectuals and those of *Season of Anomy* as "socio-active." She clarifies:

> In *The Interpreters* Soyinka projects the mainly passive intellectuals whose preoccupations are a hedonistic indulgence in self-questionings and in the exercise of their individual hobbies and interests. Their response to the hostility of their social context is an alienated withdrawal into art and a search for experience. On the other hand, Ofeyi and the Dentist of *Season of Anomy* are socio-activists who occupy themselves with schemes through which they hope to counter the offensive of the establishment in the interest of the populace.[15]

Okonkwo feels that Soyinka has given the young intellectuals the task of "understanding the shortcomings of their society" which they do by engaging themselves in the process of "clarification of very many preliminary issues."[16] To the chief characters of *Season of Anomy*, Soyinka assigns the task of taking steps "towards the achievement of . . . prescribed goal."[17] The goal is an ideal society representing the "egalitarian, morally incorruptible essence from the African past which was destroyed with the intrusion of foreign, excessively materialistic and exploitative ideologies."[18]

Though Okonkwo's analysis is a useful contribution to Soyinka scholarship, there are certain limitations to her study. She depends for her categorization of the intellectuals on an article on the influence of Western education on the psychology of its African recipients.[19] This categorization of the characters into two clear-cut groups, though convenient, is unconvincing. Specially, one cannot subscribe to Okonkwo's view that the protagonists of *The Interpreters* indulge in hedonistic pursuits and "in the exercise of their individual hobbies and interests." For such a view does not explain Sekoni's victimization by the corrupt forces and Sagoe's journalistic adventures and his zeal to expose corruption at all levels. Even the other interpreters cannot be dubbed as "passive" or "hedonists." If their encounter with the formidable exploitative forces has humbled them, it is temporary. These intellectuals are forever learning and equipping themselves with experience as part of their preparatory phase before the eruption of a revolution which materializes under the leadership of the intellectuals of *Season of Anomy*.

In an article entitled "From Social Commitment to Ideological Awareness: A Study of Soyinka's *The Interpreters* and *Season of Anomy*," Irene Assiba d'Almeida shows how the "social commitment" of Soyinka is "all pervasive" throughout his two novels. The interpreters, according to this critic, "set out to interpret their society, a society in which they feel ill at ease because of the type of values it upholds."[20] But she wonders whether these intellectuals are really committed to social change. She projects an image of the intellectuals as those dissatisfied with life, unfulfilled and those who shirk responsibility. Further, according to her, "they are all, in different ways and in various degrees, much concerned with their own development and are questioning their lives and the relevance of their lives to the society."[21] As for *Season of Anomy*, the two important characters, Ofeyi and the Dentist, are somewhat politicized. A measure of politicization is essential to bring about a positive alternative to the evils within the society. While Ofeyi "spends much time to intellectualize, to rationalize and elucidate his motives, his intentions and his actions," the Dentist carries out his "selective assassinations." The paper concludes that the Soyinkan hero, who finds himself at odds with society in *The Interpreters*, wakes up into a new awareness of his responsibility to revitalize it in *Season of Anomy*.

d'Almeida's study focuses mainly on Soyinka's purpose in analyzing and exposing the evils of Nigerian society. But she too toes essentially the same line as Okonkwo in drawing the picture of the interpreters as irresponsible youngmen engaged in their own pursuits. Such a reading of the novel leads the reader away from the truth. The novel is about the live encounter between the intellectual and society and the fruitful results of their interaction. Soyinka portrays here characters who turn inwards after confronting the formidable evil forces of the society. Making a provision for common human weaknesses, the interpreters are incorruptible and highly upright in their demeanour. Their idealism and sense of purpose are evident throughout the novel. We unmistakably find them engaged in the dual task of understanding the society while fighting its evils. Further, on account of her preoccupation with the analysis of the social issues presented in Soyinka's novels, d'Almeida seems to have neglected the important role the intellectuals play in projecting the future and shaping the course of history.

Kolawole Ogungbesan has made a study of Soyinka's novels from the point of view of the novelist's responsibility in Africa. Ogungbesan too takes the same stand as the above critics. For him, "*The Interpreters* deals with the problems of the intellectuals in the emerging African nations, a question of individual sensibility at war with the claims of society."[22] He adds by way of an explanation that Soyinka's purpose in *The Interpreters* is "to explain the status quo, not to advocate ways of changing it. By calling his central characters 'the interpreters' Soyinka is emphasizing the fact that their role is to analyse their society, not to recreate it. . . . Soyinka by analysing the prevalent mood, aimed to force society to recognize the true nature of its problems. Such recognition would be an indispensable step towards solving the problems."[23] When it came to the writing of *Season of Anomy*, "Soyinka moved from being merely the conscience of his society to being a political revolutionary."[24] In this novel he has subjugated art to social purpose and what one finds is the world of action aimed at evoking a society which is in the process of coming to birth.

Ogungbesan's article highlights those aspects of Soyinka's novels where the novelist appears to be a committed artist. Soyinka's commitment, as Ogungbesan seems to stress, does not end with an analysis of the problems facing the society. The analysis of these problems is aimed at giving his heroes the much-needed perspective for revolutionizing life and transforming society. Soyinka's real commitment is to the creation of a new and just social order for which he prepares the background in *The Interpreters*. Ogungbesan seems to have failed to see this vital link between the two novels. Further, even a cursory reading of *Season of Anomy* shows that Soyinka has not totally subjugated art to any extraneous purposes. He has successfully dealt with many social and political issues upholding all the literary values at the same time.

The above analysis shows that, perceptive and probing as the studies are, they have not been successful in getting at Soyinka's essential motive as a novelist. Nothing has been conclusively proved about Soyinka's attempt to underline the potentiality of the intellectuals who have superior knowledge and progressive ideology to lead and redeem their society. Soyinka believes that it is the supreme responsibility of the intellectuals in any society in general, and African society in particular, to interpret the present and project the future. He goes further and assigns them the task of shouldering the responsibility of leading their society towards a glorious future by their individual acts of courage as well as by mobilizing the support of the progressive forces within the society.

It can further be seen that some of these studies have treated Soyinka's intellectuals as separate entities, distinct from each other, while in fact there is a thematic progression from one to the other. It is possible to see them as different aspects of one complex intellectual hero who is truly concerned for the redemption and development of his society. Starting from Egbo, the culturally alienated hero of *The Interpreters* we can trace a gradual development of the intellectual into a full-fledged revolutionary represented by Ofeyi of *Season of Anomy*. To say that this progress closely parallels that of the "third-world intellectual" envisioned by Fanon will be perhaps a repetition.

This understanding leads me to make an attempt in this book to study the theme of the intellectual (as the most significant factor in social change) and his relation to society (which looks up to the intellectual for leadership in its process of transition) in Soyinka's fiction. The chapter on *The Interpreters* depicts the intellectuals in direct confrontation with society. This experience gives them a social vision and an ideological framework. The chapter on *Season of Anomy* highlights the attempts on the part of the intellectuals to translate their vision of ideal society into reality and the innumerable hardships they face in carrying out this great task. The Conclusion sums up the argument by comparing Soyinka's portrayal of intellectuals with those other African novelists and evaluating the actual performance of African intellectuals in a critical light. The study also examines the stylistic and structural aspects of Soyinka's works.

NOTES

1. Wole Soyinka, "This Past Must Address Its Present," *Mainstream*, No. 16, 3 Jan. 1987, p. 18.
2. Frantz Fanon, *The Wretched of the Earth*, trans. Constance Farrington (Harmondsworth: Penguin, 1982), p. 169.
3. As quoted by Ngugi wa Thiong'o, *Home Coming* (New York:

Lawrence Hill, 1972), p. 45.

4. Chinua Achebe, "The Writer and the Biafran Cause," *Morning Yet on Creation Day* (London: Heinemann, 1975), p. 82.
5. Wole Soyinka, p. 19.
6. *Ibid.*
7. Kolawole Ogungbesan, "Wole Soyinka and the Novelist's Responsibility in Africa," *New West African Literature,* ed. Kolawole Ogungbesan (London: Heinemann, 1979), pp. 7-8.
8. Frantz Fanon, p. 170.
9. *Ibid.*
10. *Ibid.*, p. 179.
11. Ngugi wa Thiong'o, p. 50.
12. Kolawole Ogungbesan, p. 5.
13. Eldred Jones, *The Writing of Wole Soyinka* (London: Heinemann, 1973), pp. 11-12.
14. Juliet Okonkwo, "The Essential Unity of Soyinka's *The Interpreters* and *Season of Anomy*," *African Literature Today*, No. 11 (1980), p. 111.
15. *Ibid.*, pp. 111-12.
16. *Ibid.*, p. 114.
17. *Loc. cit.*
18. *Ibid.*, p. 118.
19. Billiamin A. Alli, "Acculturative Forces: Nigeria in Transition," *Journal of Black Studies*, No. 4 (June 1974), p. 384.
20. Irene Assiba d'Almeida, "From Social Commitment to Ideological Awareness: A Study of Soyinka's *The Interpreters* and *Season of Anomy*." *UFAHAMU*, X, No. 3 (Spring 1981), p. 13.
21. *Ibid.*, p. 21.
22. Kolawole Ogungbesan, p. 5.
23. *Ibid.*, p. 4.
24. *Ibid.*, p. 5.

An Engagement with Reality: *The Interpreters*

On publication in 1965, *The Interpreters* received very enthusiastic reviews. Although it dealt "with the most profound experiences of . . . society,"[1] its apparent obscurity won it notoriety and critical opinion temporarily settled against the novel. The Nigerian critics, used as they were to look up to the novelist to play the teacher, condemned the book on the ground that it hardly "disturbed" anybody. Its social relevance was seriously questioned. O.O. Enekwe concluded thus: "Any work of fiction or poetry whose words are too obscure for the so-called simple, but literate, audience is not suitable for human consumption, except, perhaps, as a riddle."[2] Critic after critic has found fault with the book on various grounds, specially its complexity. William Lawson feels, "the very complexity by which Soyinka demonstrates a myriad of writing talents actually becomes an impediment. Too complex to provide a clearly perceived single experience, *The Interpreters* is a kind of compartmentalized showcase of the writer's skills."[3] Gerald Moore attributes the "difficulty" of the novel to Soyinka's inexperience as a novelist: "His relative inexperience in the art of fiction is revealed in the manner of Soyinka's opening, which requires the reader to assess and relate a number of widely different personalities who are all introduced, without history, in the first few pages of the novel."[4] And a number of readers have, according to Moore, simply "given up" as soon as they started reading the book.

One has to agree with Moore that *The Interpreters* makes compulsive reading for a greater part of its length. The reader should be prepared to get lost in the medley of incoherent details, broken chronology and multiple flashbacks which have not been, by general agreement, ably handled and hence hardly serve the purpose they are meant for. One easily perceives an inevitability when Ngugi uses flashbacks in his novels. But Soyinka has not effectively used the otherwise useful technique.

Soyinka has also taken great liberties with the language and syntax which is the main hazard to the understanding of a casual reader. James Booth observes: "Clarity of statement frequently seems less important to Soyinka than faithfulness to the complexities and ambiguities of his apprehension of life."[5] Soyinka appears to have deliberately complicated the form of the novel because he is dealing with a complex situation. Many critics and readers alike seem to have failed in penetrating the many layers of the novel's meaning.

Critics have variously stated the basic theme of *The Interpreters*. For Eldred Jones, the novel deals with the contemporary Nigerian society in which, "although the ancient traditional life still makes its appearance, the predominant impression is of a society in the grips of turbulent modernity."[6] Eustance Palmer looks at the novel as "the most comprehensive exposé of the decadence of modern African society that has so far been published."[7]

From these critical pronouncements it follows that critics have generally regarded the novel only as an authentic portrayal of the corrupt post-colonial Nigerian society. But it is more than that. Soyinka presents in this novel the corrupt, degenerate Nigerian society, which has moved away from traditional values, in order to suggest that the time is ripe for dismantling the system. He enunciates the vital role the intellectuals play in bringing about this change. The idealistic dreams of these enthusiastic young men for a rosy future in their native land are dashed to pieces by the harsh realities. Their initial reaction is one of recoil. But it does not mean that they opt out of the arena. Instead, they use this time, while licking their wounds, for penetrating the decaying pith of the society and understanding the machinations of the hostile forces operating within.

The Interpreters is a complex story of five intellectuals. Egbo, a foreign service official, Sekoni, an engineer turned sculptor, Kola, a painter and art teacher, Sagoe, a journalist, and Bandele, a university teacher, are the prominent intellectuals whom Soyinka calls "the interpreters." Soyinka's choice of the professions of these intellectuals is clear. Theirs are the most typical professions held by the intellectuals of today's Africa. Further, such a choice offers Soyinka ample scope to present life as it is lived—corrupt and hypocritical—by the elite who wield power in all spheres of Nigerian life.

These five intellectuals are highly talented and enthusiastic youngmen who are determined to make a mark in their respective fields. They are true to themselves and to each other. They are "individuals trying to make sense of their world. They are hammering out values and codes of conduct in a world which seems to have none ready made."[1] Their moral idealism, honesty and aversion to corruption leave us profoundly impressed. These qualities definitely place the interpreters above the others. Interestingly, they have all been educated in the West which necessitated their absence from home for many years. During their stay abroad they have developed a detached view of the society which, upon returning home, enables them to attempt an objective appraisal of its weaknesses and, at the same time, successfully resist its temptations. There, the interpreters gain authenticity because they themselves fall victims of the corrupt social forces on many occasions.

To appreciate their role in bringing about a positive change in the society, it is necessary that we have a fuller understanding of the post-colonial Nigerian society which is reeling under heavy Western influence and is chronically plagued by corruption. In this novel, Soyinka's penetrating eyes have torn the Nigerian society into shreds and laid bare, for our vision, the reality behind it. The universities, newspapers, religion, bureaucracy and several other major and minor institutions governing modern life become the butts of his bitter satire. One cannot overlook the fact that everything is presented to our inspection only through the discriminating eyes of these five intellectuals. Their experience of men and things makes them thoroughly disillusioned and dissatisfied with the post-colonial situation in Africa. They meticulously pinpoint the diseased state of affairs and boldly affirm the eternal and undying African values.

It is a familiar fact that African life, in the post-independence era, has become insufferable with the loss of the native cultural roots. The exploitative colonial institutions and values have been doggedly perpetuated by the black successors. Any reformative steps on the part of those who are truly concerned for their society are openly resented. People spearheading such reformation are harassed, hounded and eliminated by the repressive regimes currently ruling most African states.

In *The Interpreters*, Soyinka was chiefly preoccupied with the corruption in high places. It goes without saying that at lower levels corruption is a part of life. University life appears to be a major preoccupation of Soyinka in this novel as universities are supposed to play a significant role in a developing society and the academics, being intellectual, are expected to make their contribution to progressive social change. Contrary to these expectations, one finds much hypocrisy, pettiness and social climbing among the university group in the novel. These university dons belong to that class of intellectuals whom Paul Baran calls "intellect workers."[9] And according to Ngugi wa Thiong'o, they rationalize "a world-view or an outlook which is in harmony with the needs and positions of the dominating nation, race or class."[10] These men have easily yielded to the temptations of the corrupt society, and in course of time, become its guardians. The portrayal of the "impotent" university men is most authentic since Soyinka himself was, for many years, associated with several universities as a professor. Further, such a portrayal serves to contrast the highly upright interpreters with these shallow men and thus pinpoint their unquestionable qualification for analyzing and leading society.

Professor Oguazor's party amply offers the true picture of the life of university intellectuals. The interpreters go to attend this party and "a buzz of wit, genteel laughter and character slaughter welcomed them from the drive and they entered the house of death."[11] The shallowness and affectation of the people gathered there is emphasized by the plastic fruits that decorated Oguazor's house:

> From the ceiling hung citruous clusters on invisible wires. A glaze for the warmth of life and succulence told the story, they were the same as the artificial apples. These were fancy beach hat flowerpots on the wall, ivy clung from these along a picture rail, all plastic, and the ceiling was covered in plastic lichen. Sagoe had passed, he now noticed, under a special exhibition group of one orange, two pears, and a fan of bananas straight from European wax works. (140)

Prof. Oguazor and his wife Caroline pathetically ape outmoded British etiquette. Not wearing a neck-tie, in the sultry Nigerian climate, is frowned upon. Mrs. Oguazor is openly harsh to Monica Faseyi when she refuses to withdraw, along with other women, to privacy: "you will come with us at once . . . or don't ever expect to be invited to my house." (145) She does not pause a moment to think that this practice of the women retiring to privacy during a party is no more in fashion in England. Oguazor himself, with his affected Oxbridge accent, does not lose an opportunity to sermonize on the deterioration of moral standards among the students and teachers by citing for instance the episode of a student's premarital pregnancy. A person who appears to be so concerned about morals as to say, "The college cannot afford to have its name dragged down by the meral terpitude of irresponsible young men. The younger generation is too merally corrupt," (250) is himself guilty of "meral terpitude." The irony assumes poignancy when we are informed that Oguazor has a daughter, "the plastic apple of his eye," whom he "could not publicly acknowledge" because "he had her by the housemaid." (149) Oguazor is, however, shrewd enough to preserve his respectable facade by tucking the girl away in a private boarding school in Islington.

Ayo Faseyi, another of the university group, is an Anglomaniac who imitates the English in a servile manner. His insistence on wearing gloves in Nigeria irritates even his English wife Monica. Her preference for palm-wine at the ambassador's party greatly offends him. And the damage she caused to his social image by not obliging Mrs. Oguazor by withdrawing to privacy during the party is just irreparable. In him we have a representative of those who use the university as a springboard for entering politics and an instrument for social climbing. He explains to Bandele and Kola:

> Do you know a Minister was present. Yes, and one or two other VIPs. Oguazor knows people, you know. I saw four corporation chairmen there, and some Permanent Secretaries. . . . The university is just a stepping-stone. Politics, corporations—there is always something. Not to talk of these foreign firms, always looking for Nigerian Directors. I mean Kola, you are an artist, but I am sure it is all a means to an end, not so? (202-3)

Dr. Lumoye is yet another unscrupulous university figure who does not hesitate a moment to violate the code of professional ethics. The pregnant student who figured in their conversation earlier, approaches him for help. Besides refusing her any help, Dr. Lumoye slanders her openly:

> Well she won't get *that* kind of sympathy from me I tell you. I'm not risking seven years for someone else's pleasure. If I tasted of it myself I would at least have something to show for it. (147)

Character assassination and back-biting that these apparently respectable university men indulge in can be seen in the conversation at the Oguazor's party which is totally unbecoming of them:

> Dr. Ajilo denied that he took prostitutes home. Never further than his garage, he swore, but Oguazor was just behind him, and he was not amused.
>
> "Those madrigals. Useful grounds, you know, then the husband began to suspect the late rehearsals. . . ."
>
> "They say Mr. Udedo can't even pay his electricity bills.

> What does he do with his money?"
>
> "Who is Salubi going with these days. That boy is morally corrupt I tell you. He doesn't even keep off the students."
>
> "Wen of these days," Oguazor was saying, "the Senate will charge him with meral terpitude." (148)

The unworthiness of these shallow men to speak of morality is too evident to attract a comment. They hide their pettiness, degeneracy and preoccupation with scandals under the mantle of respectability which Soyinka brilliantly strips off through Sagoe, the journalist. Sogoe characteristically launches "savage onslaughts" on the gathering from time to time during the party by his comments and actions. His presence irritates the vicious men so much that "each guest began to ask his neighbour, "I hope it wasn't you who brought him and sighed, disappointed that the candidate had not lost his chance of nomination to some committee." (146)

Newspapers receive severe indictment from Soyinka. Though "as a crusader on social and political issues his views are frequently quoted in the press as the voice of a nascent Nigerian public opinion,"[12] Soyinka does not seem to have any sympathy for the partisan press. Considered as one of the pillars of democracy, the newspapers can do useful service to the people by placing facts before them. Though free from official curbs, the Nigerian newspapers have all the ills that characterize the third-world press. Sagoe has to bribe the board members to get a job as a journalist for the ironically named newspaper *Independent Viewpoint.* The deplorable plight of the paper is powerfully stated thus:

> [This paper] owned a large building in the slum; the paper itself was a party organ, its location meant easy patronage of local thugs. (72)

The Managing Director of the paper is an enormous figure of corruption. With his useless round-the-world economic missions and his squandering of the newspaper funds on expensive foreign goods, he is typical of the men that control the press in Nigeria. The radiogram which he picked up in Germany is hardly ever used. The real purpose behind his too frequent foreign trips is evident from his attempt to seduce the German sales-girl from whom he bought the radiogram:

> "By the way," he said, "do come to my hotel and show me how it works."
>
> "Aren't we to ship it home for you sir?"
>
> "Of course, of course," said the Director. "I meant come with the leaflets and explain it all to me; I don't read German, you see."
>
> "It is there in English also," said the girl, "and in French and Spanish and Arabic." Dragging his long trail of traditional splendour after him the Director turned to his private secretary and said, "Aren't these German girls stupid." (75)

Sir Derinola, the Chairman of the newspaper board and a respectable judge and Chief Winsala, also a member of the board, are two of those described by Sagoe as "unctuous, aggravating toads." (76) The corruption in public life is embodied in these two characters. Sir Derinola, in view of his high position in the society and the nagging fear of losing it, uses the overtly corrupt politician Chief Winsala as his front. His corruption, in association with Winsala, is particularized in the scene at the hotel where they go to collect the bribe money from Sagoe. While Sagoe is off to his room to fetch the money and Chief Winsala keeps himself busy guzzling schnapps, Sir Derin grows impatient and surreptitiously enters the hotel only to find himself face to face with Sagoe:

> Beside the young palm shoot in a halved petrol drum stood Sir Derinola. And Sagoe was never never to forget the look upon his face. Beside the fright and his affronted dignity was marked the anguish of indecision. . . . Now he saw Sagoe move forward and tried to shrink back behind the palm. They gazed into each other, all subterfuge pointless. It was Sagoe who took his eyes away. (92)

And again it was Sagoe who recoiled in embarrassment that "he should have witnessed this cruel exposure of men whose age demanded his respect." (86) As a judge, Sir Derin has allowed himself to be bought over by politicians. The prestige attached to his robes is false. So Sagoe, in his drunken stupor, imaginatively strips him naked and dresses him only in a pair of Dehinwa's brassiers while the medals that go with his knighthood hang around his neck. "The cloth does not make the man" (65) and the knighthood does not make him automatically respectable. He is what he essentially is—corrupt.

If these are the men behind the newspapers, the functioning of the otherwise most powerful democratic institution can very well be imagined. Sagoe's investigative report on the corruption involved in the scrapping of Sekoni's power plant is set aside for fear of a counter exposure. The editor of the paper explains to a disappointed Sagoe the policy pursued by the paper, "Shut your mouth, I shut mine. Plain and simple. You have got the chairman out of some nasty jam." (95) With the result, the truth never sees light. The general public is always kept in the dark. To Sagoe's protest, the editor replies: "Sagoe, look, I have been in this game for thirty years. Believe me there was a time when I held these ideals. I moved from one paper to the other, leaving in a flurry of righteous indignation. But look man, journalism here is just a business like any other. You do what your employer tells you." (95)

A glimpse of the corruption in the civil service can be had in the condemnation of the brilliant experimental power station built by Sekoni at Ijioha. The cynicism and corruption of the chairman do not allow Sekoni even to test the plant. It is condemned as junk and inoperable by a bribed "expat expert." The chairman, who has a subsidiary company registered in the name of his two-month old niece, is the sole contractor for Project Ijioha. He "cleaned out a few thousands in immediate compensation and filed claims for a few thousands more." (28) One is simply bewildered at the treatment meted out to the highly talented and imaginative engineer and the enormous waste of the precious and scarce resources of the developing nation. Instead of accelerating the country's economic development, bureaucracy has, in fact, become a serious impediment.

Religion is too closely interwoven with the lives of the Nigerians to escape Soyinka's critical treatment. Half a century or so of Christian rule has effected the conversion of a majority of the tribal idol-worshipping Nigerians to Christianity. Chinua Achebe's *Things Fall Apart* and *Arrow of God* copiously demonstrate this historical development in the spiritual life of the Nigerians. Like all the other institutions, Christianity fell into the hands of evil men and turned into a big farce. To put it in Sagoe's words, "It's good business these days, religion." (162)

It is significant to note here that Soyinka was born into a Christian family at Abeokuta. But, as he advanced in his age, he was gradually disillusioned with Christianity and finally embraced the Yoruba world-view of his forefathers. The cynicism with which Soyinka has come to view religious practices, specially those of the Christian religion and how he ridicules such mechanical religious observances, can be gathered from the conversation of Sagoe and Dehinwa who, at the time, were school-going children:

> Dehinwa asked, "Is it you spoiling the air? You have to watch them, you know. My auntie does it all the time and she blames us children. But I can always tell. I always know when she is going to do it. she bends her buttocks to one side, after that, everybody scatters."
>
> Sagoe felt superior. "My mother is more regular. Always after prayers every evening, very loud and prolonged. When the bombing is over she says, 'Thank God,' and we all have to reply, 'Amen.'" (88)

A perusal of Soyinka's works, specially his plays, reveals how impatient Soyinka is with the men that made religion serve their selfish ends. Jero of *The Trials of Brother Jero* and Professor of *The Road* are fakes that made a farce of religion. Lazarus of *The Interpreters*, a charismatic but fraudulent preacher, compels us to draw a comparison between him and the above. Critics find it "difficult to ascertain what attitude Soyinka expects us to adopt towards Lazarus and his brand of religion.''[13] Some have not hesitated to identify him with the interpreters themselves.[14] The attitude of the Christian critics has been, by and large, either one of praise for Lazarus (though with certain qualifications) or indifference. Gerald Moore, to cite an example, says:

> His [Lazarus's] methods do not differ greatly from those of any other charlatan revivalist of the Brother Jeroboam variety, but it may be that his claim to have risen from the dead is both literally bogus and imaginatively true. Or, to put it otherwise, it does not greatly matter whether it is true or not.[15]

In keeping with the general attitude of Soyinka towards various institutions throughout the novel, it may be stressed that he clearly means to condemn Lazarus and his church. The fact that Lazarus takes thieves and criminals as his apostles renders him highly questionable as "prophet." In spite of his avowed mission of saving these "fallen souls" by accepting them as his disciples, it is difficult to believe in the sincerity of his purpose. His claims of rising from the dead and turning suddenly an albino do not carry conviction. Gullible villagers that frequent his shack of a church may be carried away by his oratory and false claims, but he fails to convince the intellectuals of the significance of the service he is ostensibly rendering to society. With the exception of Bandele, the interpreters are highly critical of the man. The austerity to which Lazarus subjects the ex-thief and present-disciple Noah, evokes our unqualified sympathy. Like Christ—Lazarus identifies himself with Christ—he insists on Noah's washing the feet of the people gathered there for the Sunday service. Egbo, by flatly refusing to get his feet washed by Noah, expresses Soyinka's disapproval of such practices. The key to this interpretation lies in the fact that Egbo is the most authorial of the five important interpreters.

Lazarus does not even have a real understanding of the Bible. He makes an utter fool of himself as a result. His sermons are ridiculous in the extreme. In his harangue on how Christ won death, he says:

> He [Christ] wrestled with death and he knocked him down. Death said, let us try *gidigbo* and Christ held him by the neck, he squeezed that neck until Death bleated for mercy. But Death never learns his lesson, he went and brought boxing gloves. When Christ gave him an uppercut like Dick Tiger all his teeth were scattered from Kaduna to Aiyetoro . . . even then do you think Death would give up? Not so, my friends, not so. Death ran to his farm, took up his matchet and attacked Christ from behind. Christ dodged him like an acrobat, and then he brought out a long shining sword of stainless steel and he cut Satan's matchet in half. But he did not want to kill him altogether, so he gave him small tiny cuts all over his body and Death was walking about in bandages from head to toe like *Ologomugomu*. (165-66)

All said and done for and against Lazarus, he is shown as a big fruad, even psychotic and perhaps Soyinka means nothing less than that. The failure of Lazarus in the case of Noah who runs away from him and eventually jumps to his death, shows the transitory nature of this budding religious business. Lazarus has served Soyinka's purpose only too well. He has exemplified what damage these bogus prophets with their resurrection stories et cetera can cause to the spiritual welfare of innocent people.

This is the society in nutshell as presented in this novel by Soyinka. This society represents a new form of colonial oppression. The degeneracy of the social institutions, enumerated above, is too apparent to be emphasized. The interpreters were rightly enraged by this sad state of affairs. They had to make their best efforts to be upright and untouched by corruption themselves. So the only alternative to preserve their moral propriety and integrity is to withdraw themselves from this ''cesspool of corruption'' and launch an attack on all forms of corruption. They have undertaken this task with the understanding that the hostile forces ranged against them have to be quelled at all costs. Further, their realization of their mission has been largely unconscious. Soyinka does not state the mission of these intellectuals openly yet. We are made to understand by Soyinka's manner of presentation that these five intellectuals come to the realization only at the final stage. Before that, they go through the different stages described by Fanon for the intellectuals of pre-colonial and post-colonial society. According to Fanon, the native intellectual finds himself, at the beginning, as a culturally uprooted youngman who witnesses the victimization of his people by the oppressive establishment. He reacts to the oppression by registering his resentment and anger which, however, go unheeded. Disappointed, the intellectual makes use of his artistic endeavours to restore cultural security and confidence to his people and thus begins to associate himself closely with the masses. Finally he finds himself favourably inclined to support and be the guiding-force behind the mass upsurge. Fanon's theory seems to have inspired Soyinka as can be seen in this novel. In the following pages therefore, my endeavour will be to show how each of the interpreters approximates to the different stages, except the last one, in Fanon's formula, and consider at length certain aspects of their personality that help us understand them not only thematically but also from a human standpoint.

Critical response to the role of the intellectuals of this novel has been very unsympathetic. It has been hastily concluded that, society being what it is, the protest of the intellectuals falls on the empty air and they fail to achieve any specific ideal. And the quest of the interpreters for justice has been misinterpreted as "a search for individual solutions without the automatic props of the old sheltered way of life or any substitute for it in the modern world."[16]

William Lawson feels that the development of the theme in the novel is not logical. He appears to hold that the interpreters are flat and unchanged even at the end of the novel since in his opinion, "The view of the world that is implicit at the novel's beginning obtains at the end."[17]

Such reaction on the part of the critics was largely due to the fact that they treated the interpreters separately, highlighting their negligible weaknesses. To view the interpreters as strongly ideated characters distinct from one another is to misread the novel. A closer examination would reveal that the five interpreters are only physically separate but ideologically they constitute a single complex intellectual hero. Each character represents a different phase of the intellectual's growth. Starting from Egbo who like a typical colonial intellectual gets alienated from his people, we can trace thematic progression to Bandele who is ripe with a thorough understanding of his society and its evils.

Egbo comes first because he qualifies as a colonial intellectual who finds himself culturally alienated. Upon his return from the West, he is faced with the choice between assuming power as the traditional chief of Osa, his grandfather's kingdom, and spending an apparently inglorious and boring but secure life as a foreign service official. Egbo is aware that the foreign office job is mere "pith to hollow reeds" and that as the ruler of the Creeks Chiefdom he can do some useful service to society. In fact, the "Osa Descendants Union sent their spokesmen to plague him daily, all bitten by the bug of an enlightened ruler." (12) But his assimilation of the foreign culture is near total. He has grown to despise traditional life even if it meant power, money and women. He has been successfully weaned away from it by such powerful influences as his Western-oriented aunt who brought him up after his parents were drowned in the Creeks and his education in the West. When he is required to make the vital choice, he fails to do so and decides to go "with the tide." (14) Though he consoles himself that he has "made a choice" and that he "can't complain," he is constantly worried about his choice. Egbo's choice is a very difficult one. So Eldred Jones observes that it is a "fundamental choice involving a lot more than his personal fortunes. . . . Egbo's choice involves a break with the traditional."[15] Ill at ease in the embrace of the foreign culture, Egbo seeks security in religious mysticism and in his erotic relation with the notorious prostitute Simi.

This security is false. The intellectual is not prepared to remain forever in the domination of the foreign culture. He is jostled into a recognition of the reality when he himself becomes a victim of the evil forces of society. The suffering phase falls to Sekoni, the stammering genius. One is moved to pity by the mental torture he undergoes and by his eventual death in an accident. He has returned home from the West with very high hopes of serving his country. On his journey back home, he dreams of the magnificent things he wishes to accomplish:

> Sekoni qualified engineer, had looked over the railings every day of the sea voyage home. And the sea sprays built him bridges and hospitals, and the large trailing furrow became a deafening waterfall defying human will until he gathered it between his fingers, made the water run in the lower channels of his palm, directing it against the primeval giants on the forest banks . . . he opened his palm to the gurgle of power from the charging prisoner, shafts of power nudged the monolith along the fissures, little gasps of organic ecstasy and paths were opened, and the brooding matriarchs surrendered all their strength, lay in neat geometric patterns at his feet. Sekoni shuffled them like cards and they reshaped to magic formulae in sweeping harbours. (26)

This dream of Sekoni never comes true as he encounters the harsh realities very soon. For all his qualifications, he is assigned such trivial tasks as signing bicycle permits, looking into applications for leave of absence and so on at a routine desk position.

On his persistent request to give him a challenging assignment he is appointed the chief engineer in charge of the Ijioha power plant which he builds putting all his imagination and skill into it. But it cannot be commissioned. The chairman gets the plant scrapped as junk even before it is put into operation. Sekoni, sensitive as he is, finds the humiliation and disappointment too much to bear. Thoroughly frustrated, he batters the plant with his own hands and goes mad.

The degradation Sekoni suffers justifiably earns the wrath of the intellectual that Sagoe is. He is gravely offended. In his own way Sagoe attempts to avenge the injustice done to Sekoni. Sagoe is the most realistic of all the interpreters. With his philosophy of shift "voidancy," he lashes at the corrupt forces. He explains:

> Voidancy is not a movement of protest, but it protests: it is non-revolutionary, but it revolts. Voidancy—shall we say—is the unknown quantity. Voidancy is the uncharted mine of creative energies, in its paradox lies the kernel of creative liturgy—in release its birth. (71)

Though somewhat repugnant to our sense of decency, the "philosophy" deserves credit for its excremental vision of life which today's Nigerian life necessitates. Voidancy is just inches short of Swift's misanthropy projected in Houyhnhnmanland. The key of this interpretation is in Sagoe's report on human excrement strewn in a city street the photographs of which could not be published for it would "offend the readers." But neither the authorities nor the general public appear to be bothered about it. The heap lies in the street for days on end, infesting the area with unbearable stench and disease. The indifference of Nigerians to shit and stench in the street suggests their apathy to corruption in their society. From the days of his constipated childhood, Sagoe has never left his preoccupation with this view of life.

Sagoe is also indignant of the foreigners operating in his country and he makes no secret of it. Talking to Peter, the German journalist, he vehemently asserts: "Drive them out, drive them out, who the hell do they think they are, how dare they abuse our sovereign integrity with neo-colonialist neo-capitalist reactionary misrepresentation, deport the bastards." (136)

In Sekoni's case, however, he fails. His "two weeks of murderous work" on preparing a report on Sekoni's condemned power plant ironically serves to save the face of the corrupt Derinola. Sagoe in an apparent displacement of his anger and helplessness, complains to the office-boy Mathias, "Silence, Mathias. Silence. I have known all kinds of silence, but it's time to learn some more." (98) His failure in itself is not important. That he has the nerve to protest is a point to be considered seriously. The intellectual in Sagoe has realized the inadequacy of mere protest to effect any substantial change in society. It is only through a mass movement backed by a time-tested ideology that society can see deliverance from its present filth and squalor. The people have to be awakened to the reality of the situation. They have to be convinced of the richness of their past. The intellectual has now to revive some of the forgotten cultural norms. Significantly, Kola, who is the artistic self of the complex intellectual hero, sets aside Christianity as inadequate and unsuitable for this purpose. He will become another Lazarus if he views Christianity as being capable of raising the consciousness of the people. Instead, he delves deep into his people's distant past which he appears to believe to have the potentiality to offer a solution to the present-day problems if it is reinterpreted so as to meet the challenges of modern life to produce most salutory effects. Kola may be said to have fulfilled what Fanon expects of the intellectual at this stage. Fanon says: "[the intellectual] uses the past with the intention of opening the future, as an invitation of action and a basis for hope."[19] To his great delight he discovers in the past "nothing to be ashamed of but rather dignity, glory and solemnity."[20]

Kola's preoccupation throughout the novel is with his Pantheon. Though doubts about the significance of the Pantheon have been voiced, Soyinka's purpose behind it could be none other than the revival of the past of the oppressed people in artistic terms and thus remind them of their rich cultural heritage. The fact that Kola has chosen to paint a galaxy of the presiding Yoruba deities, with special emphasis on Ogun, Soyinka's favourite god, speaks volumes for the intellectual's attempt to reinterpret his culture using modern devices with the aim of restoring cultural identity and the security that goes with it, to his people. When looked at from this angle, Kola's artistic preoccupation becomes more a kind of cultural elixir rather than a means of escape.

Attempts to revive the forgotten culture and traditional mores have been made elsewhere in the novel by the intellectuals. Egbo's preference for palm wine, their unqualified enjoyment of the traditional *apala* band at the night-club and the ritualistic killing of a black ram to mark the opening of Sekone's art exhibition, along with Kola's Pantheon, can be interpreted as powerful assertion of the contemporary relevance and significance of the cultural practices which suffered near-extinction with the advent of the colonial domination. With this, the first two important phases of the intellectual's growth come to an end.

The methods employed by them so far, be it the hysterical outbursts of Sagoe or the revivalist artistic endeavours of Kola to effect social change of a kind, are unsatisfactory and extremely limited in their scope. Hence they have proved ineffective. The intellectual will eventually realize that "muscular action" should replace itself for ineffective methods for which he has to align himself with the struggle of the people. As Fanon would have it the native intellectual, one with the artistic sensibility of Kola for example, wishing to create an authentic work of art should realize that "the truths of a nation are in the first place its realities. He must go on until he has found the seething pot out of which the learning of future would emerge."[21]

It is therefore now high time for the intellectual to equip himself with a sound ideology as the first step to a sweeping social change. But even before that he should be confident of the thoroughness of his understanding of his society. Bandele represents this very important phase of the intellectual's mental make-up. Though we are kept in the dark about his past since the very beginning, we find that he has conducted himself with dignity and grace. Jones rightly remarks: "He [Bandele] is the embodiment of Soyinka's positive values."[22] Besides correcting the erring interpreters on many occasions, Bandele authentically interprets the present with his "very passivity and . . . quite insistence upon connecting people."[23] His eventual estrangement from the rest of the group symbolizes the intellectual's dissociation from his former immature self. He needs time to think and understand himself and his society better. Sitting "like a timeless image brooding over lesser beings," (244) he pronounces the final and profound curse on the corruptors of the society: "I hope you all live to bury your daughters." (251) And with that the intellectual is off to his ideological world. It cannot yet be said that Bandele has emerged as a revolutionary. This phase of the struggle is depicted in Soyinka's second novel *Season of Anomy*, in which the intellectual

Ofeyi dedicates himself for the cause of his people as a participant in and an ardent supporter of people's revolutionary movement.

Many African critics have expressed their dissatisfaction with the ending of the novel. They are critical of Soyinka for depicting the intellectuals as flat and spineless men chiefly occupied with their personal problems and pursuits. For instance, Ngugi concludes that Soyinka draws a static picture of the intellectuals in *The Interpreters*. He feels that Soyinka should not satisfy himself with highlighting the weaknesses of his society by exposing it in breadth but he "must go beyond this, to seek out sources.... By diving into its sources he can give a moral direction and vision to a struggle which, though suffering temporary reaction, is continuous and is changing the face of the twentieth century."[24] On a closer reading of the novel, however, one can discover ample evidence to the contrary. Soyinka's conception of society has always been dynamic and there has come about a definite change in the intellectuals. There is a sense of awakening in them followed by an awareness of the issues involved. The path they choose for the actualization of their dream of a better social order becomes the subject of his second novel in which the intellectual hero is portrayed as a political revolutionary. *The Interpreters* forms only a part of Soyinka's political-cum-social vision. He employs a complex narrative style, which has many reasonances, to present this vision. A discerning reader has to look for what is suggested than what is stated. Perhaps it is only then, that the real success behind the intellectuals's apparent failure becomes clear. We find them greatly changed at the end which is suggested but not openly stated. If they grow silent at the end it is an ominous silence which has all the portents of a brewing storm.

NOTES

1. Kolawole Ogungbesan, "Wole Soyinka and the Novelist's Responsibility in Africa," *New West African Literature*, ed. Kolawole Ogungbesan (London: Heinemann, 1979), p. 8.

2. O.O. Enekwe, "Wole Soyinka as a Novelist," *Okike* (1975), p. 76, quoted by Kolawole Ogungbesan, p. 8.
3. William Lawson, *The Western Scar: The Theme of Been-to in the West African Fiction* (Ohio: Ohio University Press, 1982), p. 97.
4. Gerald Moore, *Wole Soyinka* (London: Evans Brothers, 1971), p. 79
5. James Booth, "The Artist and Political Commitment: Wole Soyinka," *Writers and Politics in Nigeria* (London: Hodder and Stoughton, 1981), p. 114.
6. Eldred Jones, *The Writing of Wole Soyinka* (London: Heinemann, 1973), pp. 162-63.
7. Eustance Palmer, *The Growth of the African Novel* (London: Heinemann, 1979), p. 241.
8. Eldred Jones, p. 156.
9. Paul Baran, "The Commitment of the Intellectual," *Intellectual and the "Left" in Africa,* No. 32 (April 1985), p. 47.
10. Ngugi wa Thiong'o, "The Commitment of the Intellectual," in interview with Obi Bini, *Intellectual and the "Left" in Africa,* No. 32 (April 1985), p. 19.
11. Wole Soyinka, *The Interpreters* (London: Heinemann, 1970), p. 139.
12. James Booth, p. 123.
13. Eustance Palmer, p. 263.
14. Gakwandi considers Lazarus one of the interpreters, a view endorsed by James Booth, pp. 141-42.
15. Gerald Moore, p. 85.
16. Eldred Jones, p. 166.
17. William Lawson, pp. 97-98.
18. Eldred Jones, p. 156.
19. Frantz Fanon, *The Wretched of the Earth*, p. 187.
20. *Ibid.*, p. 169.
21. *Ibid.*, p. 181.
22. Eldred Jones, p. 252.
23. Gerald Moore, p. 80.
24. Ngugi wa Thiong'o, *Home Coming* (New York: Lawrence Hill, 1973), p. 66.

Never Too Late to Regain Paradise: *Season of Anomy*

Season of Anomy appeared in 1973, nearly eight years after *The Interpreters*. In the meantime the social and political situation on the African continent had greatly deteriorated and it seemed to set the stage for the emergence of a novel like the present one. Eustance Palmer observes on the situation:

> To many, it seemed that the continent was retrogressing to a state of barbarism where the ordinary human being was deprived of all rights and his life was of no account to the authorities. . . . The immediate post-indepedence phase of social and political corruption and intellectual dishonesty was now giving way to a bleaker phase of dictatorship, victimization, thuggery and violence organized occasionally at the highest level, and prevailing atmosphere of fear.[1]

Nigeria, for its part, had experienced two military coups in quick succession involving great bloodshed. The second coup had led to a large-scale violence among the civilian population. Thousands of Ibos were massacred in northern Nigeria. Such an outbreak of violence is attributed largely to the hatred of the establishment for the Ibos, because within a short period of time after independence they emerged as the most politically active and economically sound elements of the Nigerian society. Soyinka was deeply disturbed by the fact that two sections of his own society should so fight for material considerations. In response, he did what was characteristically and naturally expected of him. In spite of being a Yoruba himself, Soyinka immediately launched a travel tour of the disturbed areas to bring about a reconciliation between the Federal

Military Government and the rebel Biafram Forces. During one such journey he was attacked but he narrowly escaped death. His efforts were, however, misinterpreted and he was forced to spend a little over two years in solitary confinement. *Season of Anomy* was written while he was still serving this prison term. It is believed that he wrote the novel between the lines of two books lent, in violation of rules, by a gaol warden who happened to be his admirer. The novel's setting is unmistakably based on the situation in Nigeria in 1966 when most of the massacres took place. Soyinka was deeply distressed not only by the atrocities he had been a witness to, but also his unjust internment. His experiences at the prison have been recorded in his powerful prison diary *The Man Died* which is relevant to this study in so far as it provides an authentic background against which *Season of Anomy* was written. Soyinka's "personal vengeance [against his captors] translates into a commitment to justice, not only for a specific society but also for humanity at large, and assumes some ideological dimension in the novel which issued from the same context and inspiration."[2]

A lot of thinking seems to have gone into the making of *Season of Anomy*. Soyinka's civil war experiences were still very fresh in his mind. Highly disturbed as he was, Soyinka delved deep into the society in this novel to reach the roots of the problems facing it and he realized the necessity of a radical approach to solve them. Commenting on this aspect of the novel, James Booth observes:

> Soyinka's treatment indicates that the real sources of tension within society are not the apparent ones of regionalism and atavism. These are merely tools in the hands of class interests. In Soyinka's version the outbreak of tribalism in the Northern massacres is in fact a deliberately orchestrated diversionary tactic, used by the alliance of military government and bourgeoisie for their own material ends.[3]

Without many exceptions critics have agreed that the chief concern of the novel is Soyinka's increasing support to revolutionary action, the undercurrents of which are easily discernible throughout the book. Emmanuel Ngara states:

> The theme of the novel is based on the dialectical relationship between exploitation and revolution, and Soyinka points to the inevitability of violence as a method of bringing about justice to the oppressed peoples of Africa. For thinking people like Ofeyi [the hero] the prevailing social conditions present a serious challenge. But the challenge applies no less to Soyinka than it does to Ofeyi, for Soyinka is certainly becoming a militant writer.[4]

Significance of the change in Soyinka's stance from contemplation to commitment to revolutionary action can be realized fully when we read *Season of Anomy* as a depiction of the second phase, the revolutionary phase, of his social and political vision. Soyinka is very explicit about his political commitment in *Season of Anomy*. There is a marked shift in his attitude towards the relation between the intellectual-activist and the public in this novel. Commenting on this shift, James Booth says: "The pessimistic retreat into the private-self found in *The Interpreters* has been superseded by an energetic attempt to realize his 'social potential,' to forge a practical rationale for revolutionary action."[5]

One has no quarrel with the critics considered above about the chief preoccupation of Soyinka in this novel. By the time he came to write *Season of Anomy*, Soyinka had indeed become a militant writer with his ever-increasing commitment to society. In his own way, as Booth adumbrates, Soyinka may be said to have reached the third phase, the "fighting phase" of Fanon, with a call to arms in this novel. But we feel the urge to disagree with most of the critics when it comes to Soyinka's manner of treating his theme. The theme of the intellectual's social commitment is clearly brought over from *The Interpreters* and treated to its end in the present novel. This thematic link between the two novels has not been fully realized by many. The composite intellectual hero of *The Interpreters* has stopped at the stage of being a nascent revolutionary, in close conformity with Fanon's formula, waiting for the situation to become ripe. Soyinka has, in the light of the adverse turn history took, perhaps felt then that it was high time for his intellectual to leave aside his dilemmas, paradoxes and vacillations and come out openly committed to the cause of his society. Eventually in this novel, the man of the ideas stops being merely the conscience of his society and gets positively involved in the struggle for liberation of the enslaved spirits of his people. This is precisely what we find in Ofeyi and even more in the Dentist of *Season of Anomy*. The occasional intellectualization and rationalization of situation, so typical of intellectuals, have not left Ofeyi for good yet. It is only the Dentist who qualifies as a full-fledged revolutionary in the sense in which Fanon views an African intellectual. But most of the events in the novel are viewed through the consciousness of Ofeyi and again it is Ofeyi who is ready with an alternative once the present system is demolished. The Dentist has no such vision. He envisages nothing beyond violence and elimination of the enemy. He clarifies his stance to Ofeyi at one point: "Don't ask me what I envisage. Beyond the elimination of men I know to be destructively evil, I envisage nothing. What happens after is upto people like you."[6]

Ofeyi first snaps his contacts with the corrupt establishment and after passing through several phases of experience concedes to the use of violence for realizing the ideal he has accepted from the Aiyero community. He finds no other method effective. That Soyinka has adopted a revolutionary attitude is beyond dispute. Ofeyi's approval of violence seems to be a natural outcome of the changed attitude of Soyinka.

What warranted this change in Soyinka can be understood well only against the background of the social and political turmoils most faithfully relived in this novel. A dozen or so years of independence have reduced the Nigerian social scene to a deplorable state. The corrupt forces which drove the intellectuals to the point of despair in *The Interpreters* are now centred in one organization, "the Cartel." Apparently the Cartel is only a cocoa corporation, but it is all-powerful. All the forces of exploitation and oppression have merged into its making. It is typical of the multinationals holding the former colonies in an economic stranglehold. The Cartel's four pillars represent four important wings of the establishment. Chief Batoki is the Western governor and the brain of the corporation. Zaki Amuri is the Northern traditional leader and a deadly designer. The commandant-in-chief of the armed forces symbolizes the backing of the military to the sinister organization. And Chief Biga is the "Muscle Quota" of the Cartel. The Cartel does not confine its activities to the economic exploitation of the masses. Its patronizers have their interests too. It has to ensure that the military junta perpetuates its undemocratic rule and that the activities of the chiefs should go unscathed. Further, the Cartel is quick to realize that its power is not based on the will of the people which makes it highly suspicious of those disagreeing with its wishes. The spread of the traditional but progressive Aiyero ideal gravely threatens its interests in the Cross-river province. So the Cartel unleashes a reign of terror in a desperate attempt to stop the spread of the ideal. Soyinka takes us through a series of massacres and atrocities, committed without remorse, by the denizens of the Cartel. By such a kaleidoscopic vision of the deterioration of the political situation and the security environment in Nigeria, we understand not only what necessitated Soyinka's changed outlook but also the sinister methods adopted by the Cartel in protecting its interests.

Zaki Amuri wants a clean sweep of the aliens, the Aiyero men in Cross-river. The Aiyero cadres have already established their roots in the area. The Aiyero idea could be killed, Amuri hopes, by exterminating the men spreading it. With the implicit support of the law-enforcing agencies, he inflicts untold suffering on the aliens in Cross-river. The famous church massacre, for instance, speaks volumes about the Zaki's devilish designs. During a respite from curfew the Aiyero people at Kuntua go to attend a Sunday service. The white-robed Moslems, instigated by the Zaki, storm the church armed with crude weapons and kerosene cans. They seal the gates and after dowsing the building in kerosene set it ablaze. The people caught in the fire make a desperate attempt to break loose and run to safety. Here is a passage describing their pathetic struggle between life and death.

> It was a moment the attackers had awaited. As the first man leapt out an arrow flew towards the flames, transfixed him briefly. The figure staggered, recovered balance and fled towards imagined safety. More followed him, and so did the steady procession of arrows, thudding into their targets and wringing execrations from their lips. The last man turned, pulling at the shaft embedded in his throat and, crazed by the pain tried to clamber back into the inferno. Another arrow struck him in the spine and he shuddered, fell over the sill and hung there as flames licked his clothes and soon engulfed him completely. (195)

Significantly the police personnel posted there callously withdraw from the place. One is not "certain which was the least menace, the murderous squads which roamed about at will . . . or the police." (254)

Such outbreak of violence has led to a revival of atavistic tribalism. In his search for his girl friend Iriyise, who has been abducted by the Cartel, Ofeyi encounters a group of tribals hunting down a helpless fugitive. The victim throws himself against his car. He is first mistaken for a monkey. While Ofeyi stands at a safe distance, unable to decide what to do, the tribals emerge from the bushes armed with matchets. There is total absence of hatred on their faces. They kill the fugitive with almost ritualistic perfection and piety:

> The varnished skull of one—he seemed to be the oldest among them—rose above the others and his mouth moved, shedding what seemed to be a brief devotional fragment on the scene. Then someone unsheathed a dagger, placed it in his hand. It rose, glinted briefly in the sun and the old man stooped and drew it across the throat of the prostrate figure.
>
> His hand moved again, this time down the body, the knife-tip drew a swift, practised circle on the crotch and his other

> hand held up the victim's genitals. He passed it to one of the many eager hands which also uselessly held open a jaw that had opened wide to thrust out pain. Into that mouth they stuffed his penis with the testicles. Then they all stepped back and looked on the transformation they had wrought. (159)

Ofeyi's reaction to such gross disrespect to human life is one of nauseating hatred and near mad frenzy. The paralysis laid on him by mutilation and slaughter cannot be shaken unless the fugitive is avenged. With that "frantic resolve" Ofeyi repeatedly rams his car into the group of the tribals killing one of them on the spot. Zaccheus, his companion, has to make a desperate appeal to Ofeyi's good sense to restore "a measure of normality," to him. Such quick and violent response is unusual on Ofeyi's part, especially since he is not convinced of the necessity of violence for social change as yet.

The Cartel is not satisfied with the terrorizing of the peace-loving populace. Its corrupting power is beyond limits. It has successfully corrupted all the men associated with it. The cocoa chairman's party exemplifies the hypocrisy of the high society and the criminal waste of resources of the young nation. The installation of the statue of St. George with his horse trampling a dragon at the chairman's house is completely out of place in Nigeria and it shows the tasteless extravagance of the chairman. His speech at the unveiling ceremony, besides being artificial and hypocritical, brings out the subtle irony involved in the Cartel's relationship with the Nigerians:

> "We all know the story of St. George and the dragon I think" the Chairman expounded as the applause rose and fell and the oh-ahs quietened. "Well, you may not guess that what I have done here is to put it to symbolical use. Which is why I specially hoped that one of our new rulers would be able to unveil the master-piece in person. St. George seated on that horse there as you can see is representative of the new order which is battling the dragon which represents the forces of our greatest national enemy—corruption!" (42)

The chairman himself is an embodiment of corruption and the "new rulers" he refers to, obviously the military, are no exception. It is sheer hypocrisy of the chairman which makes him speak the way he does. One is immediately reminded of Prof. Oguazor of *The Interpreters* and his party to faculty members. The St. George statue appears to imply deeper things than what the chairman hypocritically says. A different version of the "symbolical use" to which Soyinka perhaps puts St. George, his horse and the dragon is this: St. George represents the British national pride. If his statue evokes great awe and respect from the upper-class Nigerians, it only speaks for their servile attitude towards the British. St. George rides a horse which may symbolize the European economic enslavement of Nigeria and the dragon he kills can possibly be the progressive, hence rebellious, elements to Nigerian society who are currently being hounded and killed by the Cartel wolves.

On the political front the Cartel has "Jeku," the party it patronizes and manipulates. Jeku exemplifies how the Cartel uses political parties to further its interests. Jeku, in turn, manipulates others to achieve its own ends. Soyinka skillfully brings out this chain process through the episode of the corrupt judge who has stooped lower than Sir Derinola of the earlier novel. The Dentist pursues and eliminates this judge for the injustice he has done to his people at the instance of Jeku:

> In those early days, at the commencement of his sanctification of crimes from the bench, even, of murder, obeying a call on the telephone or a whisper from the leader of Jeku he had earned the inevitable name of Daddy Cowboy—a gun had fallen from his pocket at a public function and the guests roared with laughter at his clumsy efforts to retrieve it and return it into his pocket. (111)

In one word there is not a single institution that the Cartel leaves out. Its corrupting influence is all-pervasive. Soyinka appears to have put the very idea of the Cartel to a symbolic use. The

Cartel stands for the "establishment" with the many evils attending on it. In reality, there is no organization in Nigeria bearing even remote similarity to Cartel. Freely using his fictional license, Soyinka has clarified the Nigerian reality. Much of the artistic effect and compactness of the novel depend on such convenient tools employed by the author as we shall see.

This is the tension-charged and violence-ridden social situation the intellectual confronts in *Season of Anomy*. The intellectual, Ofeyi, is very much a part of the Cartel and thus the establishment in the beginning. At the opening of the novel, we find him as the chief promotions officer for the Cocoa Marketing Board of the Cartel. His publicity campaign takes him to an ideal township called Aiyero. The Aiyero society objectifies the kind of society the intellectual has all along been visualizing. His absorption into the Aiyero society is sudden, complete and permanent. What Aiyero represents is, however, not openly stated. In his characteristic way Soyinka drops only a few hints here and there leaving much to the imagination of the reader. We are required to carefully construct the Aiyero ideal from the novel.

The Aiyero community is a break-away group of a larger Christian community, Aiyetomo. They have split on the question of religion. It is possible to interpret this development as the Aiyero community's dislike for Christianity which was forcibly thrust on the Nigerians by the colonialists. Pa Ahime, who was the Chief Minister of the Custodian of the Grain, explains to Ofeyi:

> one day one of our young men had this thought. He told himself, we base our lives on the teachings of this white god yet the bearers of that faith kill, burn, maim, loot and enslave our people. It is time, he said, to return to the religion of our fathers (10)

And the founder of Aiyero, the first Custodian of the Grain, "gave voice to his new-found faith. He set off to found a new homeland, and those who believed him followed him." (9) Thus Aiyero was born. But Aiyero has never snapped its umbilical cord with the parent community. The Aiyero people tell their young ones of their past without colouring it with their prejudices. According to Ahime, the first Custodian of the Grain founded Aiyero "to seek truth, a better life, all the things which men run after." (9)

Critics have offered varied interpretations of the Aiyero ideal. Gerald Moore, for example, says Aiyero is "communistic ... in the sense that every freeborn son was entitled to the land he could farm—not necessarily the same amount as his neighbour—and that the wealth which accrued to the Oba and the chief was consumed within the community, much of it in the form of hospitality to the citizens. . . . Soyinka's dream if presumably of a state made up of many small communal units, each resembling Aiyero."[7] For Eustance Palmer, Aiyero society is "vibrantly life affirming, [with] the need for a commitment of truth and a better life . . . the inhabitants of Aiyero affirm their vigorous commitment to life."[8] Juliet Okonkwo has said, "Aiyero represents . . . the egalitarian, morally incorruptible essence from the African past,"[9] which was destroyed in course of time by foreign intruders and exploitative ideologies.

It follows, therefore, that Aiyero is a quasi communalistic and quasi communistic village state. It would be equally true to view Aiyero as Soyinka's answer to the radical communist utopian ideal envisaged by Ngugi wa Thiong'o, Ousmane Sembene and others. The material and spiritual welfare of every member of the community is well looked after under the able leadership of the Custodian of the Grain. The word "Grain" has no religious connotations. To put it in simple words, the Aiyero ideal is "only a way of life . . . a philosophy." (1) The community has its observances and rituals too. These rituals show how the Aiyero people live in close affinity with earth and the value they ascribe to their relationship to nature. On the death of the Custodian of the Grain, Pa Ahime explains to Ofeyi:

> We are farming and fishing community so we acknowledge our debts to earth and to the sea. And when a great man dies, a founder, we pay him homage. If we wish to take one full year

> burying him it is still less than his due. For a people who own everything in common what we spend merely returns to us. (11)

And fourteen noble bulls are sacrificed in honour of the Custodian of the Grain who has died after naming Ofeyi his successor.

The Aiyero men, spread far and wide on the globe, do not get enslaved by the attractions of the big cities. They realize that the Aiyero ideal is superior to what they see and experience elsewhere. So they keep in constant touch with their parent community as long as they are away, and in the end, they inevitably return home. Their surplus incomes go into the coffers of Aiyero. They remain so attached and upright because "they live by an idea, their lives are bound up by the one idea . . . they cannot be corrupted, or swayed." (27) The Aiyero ideal transcends the narrow confines of the ethnic group by virtue of its universal validity. It is no wonder then that the ways of Aiyero "have always been the dream of mankind all through the ages and among people . . . far apart." (12) Soyinka opens the novel with a passage that shows how the Aiyero life is lived in practice:

> A quaint anomaly, had long governed and policed itself, was so singly-knit that it obtained a tax assessment for the whole populace and paid it before the departure of the pith helmeted assessor, in cash, held all property in common, literally, to the last scrap of thread on the clothing of each citizen—such an anachronism gave much patronizing amusement to the cosmopolitan sentiment of a profit-hungry society. A definitive guffaw from the radical centres of debate headed by Ilosa, dismissed Aiyero as the prime example of unscientific communalism, primitive and embarrassingly sentimental. To the governments that came and went it posed neither threat nor liability. Thus it was that Aiyero, unique beneficiary of a three-quarter century of accidental isolation was permitted to be itself. (2)

The Aiyero ideal has stayed put for a long time until its discovery by Ofeyi. The sons of Aiyero do not believe in evangelizing the ideal as they consider evangelism a form of aggression. Consequently the task of perfecting and spreading the ideal across the country is laid on the shoulders of the intellectual Ofeyi who is an outsider. Ofeyi realizes that "the waters of Aiyero need to burst their banks. The grain must find new seminal grounds or it will atrophy and die." (6) The Aiyero ideal should not be allowed to die at any cost as it represents the best of the African past and that modern life can "only recover its meaning and its soul by a full-hearted espousal of African values and civilization."[10]

Ofeyi's transformation is instantaneous, indicating that Soyinka's intellectual hero has now emerged from his inner sanctuary as he has the cause for fighting set before him in all solidity. That Aiyero holds an irresistible attraction to all the basically good people is evident from Iriyise's example. Aiyero makes a deep and profound impression on her. This fact assumes significance because uptill now her "only knowledge of fulfilment . . . had been the aftermath of love." On staying for some days at Aiyero she declares, "it filled me Ofe, it filled me completely where I had felt so empty. I know I am now complete." (7) Iriyise immediately abandons "the circuit of Ilosa's lights, the earth of Aiyero held her deeper than any bed of eiderdown" and "from merely singing praises of 'cocoa complexion' she had burgeoned in unforeseeable directions." (20)

Once thoroughly absorbed into the Aiyero community and engrossed with the idea of distributing the fruits of the idea represented by it, Ofeyi promptly throws the cocoa publicity campaign to the winds and takes to the spreading of the Aiyero ideal. He accepts the leadership of the Aiyero community as desired by the Custodian of the Grain, though no formal ceremony is performed to celebrate the occasion, and for all practical purposes becomes the "Custodian of the Grain." He is given the full charge of Aiyero men there and elsewhere. At first he tries peaceful ways of transforming the Aiyero society and the surrounding areas with Shage as the border, for he still believes that passive methods can work. A power station and a cocoa farm are started at Aiyero to ensure economic security to the township. The Aiyero men start experimental farms in the Cross-river area. They organize the workers at Shage dam on the communist lines which means that they "could start with newly created working communities. New affinities, working-class kinships as opposed to the tribal." (165) They kill "the atavistic instinct once for all in new ventures like Shage." (165) Besides looking after the material welfare of the adherents of the ideal, the Shage also serves to explain that the Aiyero men have become politically active and organized. Now the goals are clear enough to Ofeyi. The drama of a new "concept of labouring hands" across artificial frontiers, "the concrete, affective presence of Aiyero" throughout the land is very much a reality. These organized workers have in them the confidence of undermining "the Cartel's superstructure of robbery, indignities and murder, ending the new phase of slavery." (27)

Ofeyi, who is still in charge of the Cartel's publicity campaign, hopes to defeat it by its own publicity method. If with his genius and poetry he can promote the sale of adulterated cocoa, he can as well pay the Cartel's deception in the same coin. He begins composing satirical poems to start with:

> They milked the cocoa-tree in a mass operation
> They drained the nectar, peeled the gold
> The trees were bled prematurely old
> Nor green nor gold remained for the next generation. (33)

This poem is supposed to be a cautionary tale against over-planting the land, but the reference is quite obvious. If Nigerian economy and manpower are symbolized by the cocoa tree, the Cartel has sucked it dry. This disguised insult in Ofeyi's song has not escaped the notice of the chairman of the cocoa board.

As time passes Aiyero, once the "comic Utopia," becomes "a moral thorn in the complacent skin of the national body." (82) The Cartel with its "long tentacles" loses no time in tracing the genesis of the movement to Aiyero. Its bosses are even aware that Ofeyi is the main pillar of support to Aiyero men. But the corporation is not prepared to lose Ofeyi as he happens to be its most successful promotions officer. It hopes that Ofeyi's absence from home can easily cripple the movement. So he is sent on a "study tour" of the West where he comes into contact with Demakin the Dentist who, together with Ofeyi, gives a new dimension and thrust to the Aiyero struggle at a later stage. The Dentist as we have seen is an advocate of violence through and through. It is only long after that we learn that Ofeyi's meeting with the Dentist is not accidental. It has been arranged by Pa Ahime, for the Dentist too is a son of Aiyero. Ofeyi's belief so far that passive resistance to the exploitation of the Cartel exemplified by his satirical poems does not satisfy Pa Ahime. Being essentially a man of the mind, Ofeyi needs to convince himself of the rationale behind constructively using violence to counter the Cartel on every front. Perhaps it is with this idea—to wean Ofeyi away from his non-violent methods—that Pa Ahime brought the Dentist and Ofeyi together.

The Cartel is disappointed to find no change in Ofeyi upon his return. He is called upon to give an explanation of his highly questionable behaviour while still in the employ of the Corporation. The Cartel's frenzied reaction appears to be quite in keeping with Fanonian thought. Where colonial situation prevails, says Fanon,

> Every native won over, every native who had taken the pledge not only marks a failure for the colonial structure when he decides to lose himself and go back to his own side, but also stands as a symbol for the uselessness and the shallowness of all the work that has been accomplished. Each native who goes back over the line is a radical condemnation of the methods of the regime; and the native intellectual finds in the scandal he gives rise to a justification and an encouragement to persevere in the path he has chosen.[11]

In choosing to "go back to his own side," Ofeyi appears to not only inflict a severe blow on the Cartel but also finds more than a "justification" to persevere in the path laid down by the Aiyero model, for it is in the interest of the whole nation. Interestingly therefore it is a government trouble-shooter that tries him, implying that the government too is deeply disturbed by, and has started taking serious note of, his activities. The spread of the Aiyero ideal obviously means losing the government's grip over the people. The trouble-shooter's remarks at the interrogation reveal how jittery the Cartel and the government are at the progress of the movement:

> The Commandant of the region is personally interested in this case. He considers it his duty to step in when a crisis threatens more than the immediate parties of the crisis. . . . The country's economic health is affected. Your activities Mr. Ofeyi, have begun to cause both the Corporation and the Government very great concern. (50-51)

The above passage also proves how all the agencies of oppression are hand in glove with the Corporation.

At this trial, Ofeyi shows the first signs of the pent-up hatred for the Cartel in him. He comes out with an open advocacy of the cause of the workers, knowing fully well that such championing of their cause right in the midst of the Cartel jackals will endanger his personal safety: "What we don't know is where the workers disappear to, the so-called agitators." (52) With this, the flimsy thread that held him bound to the Corporation is permanently snapped. By tendering his resignation, Ofeyi symbolically frees himself from all forms of bondages with the corrupt establishment. His next step will be to devote himself, body and soul, to Aiyero ideal and its spreading with the active support of his faithful followers and of such others who are ideologically one with him.

But the Cartel is bent upon destroying the ideal, now that it has openly challenged its might and has become a threat to its very existence. The Corporation strongly hopes that by diverting the attention of Ofeyi, the brain of Aiyero, to something else, it can weaken the struggle and finally win the battle. The result is the abduction of Iriyise to whom Ofeyi has been emotionally attached. The Cartel does succeed in its endeavour to some extent. Ofeyi, deeply involved as he is with the struggle all along, now gets occupied with his search for Iriyise. From this point onwards, Soyinka puts Ofeyi-Iriyise relationship on a symbolic plane. Their relation closely resembles that of Orpheus and Eurydice of the Greek myth. While Orpheus fails in winning back Eurydice for whatever reason, Ofeyi succeeds in rescuing Iriyise marking a break with the mythical frame given to their relationship. Iriyise has stayed at Aiyero only for a brief period during the cocoa campaign. In such a short time, she has come to mean so much to the Aiyero people that the Aiyero women boast that her presence "inspired the rains." (20) No wonder then that the Aiyero ideal is personified by Iriyise. Her loss will be a setback, even defeat, to the ideal. She has to be traced and rescued if the Aiyero ideal is to live and perpetuate. Ofeyi explains what deeper things the search for Iriyise means to him:

> I'm sure every man feels the need to seize for himself the enormity of what is happening, of the time in which it is happening. Perhaps deep down I realize that the search would immerse me in the meaning of the event, lead me to a new understanding of history. (213)

Meanwhile, not satisfied with the abduction of Iriyise, the Cartel lets loose violence on a large scale. Terror, victimization, murder and mutilation are openly perpetrated, in blatant violation of all norms of security with the active support of the blood-thirsty military rulers. But, the Aiyero people having become politically fully conscious, doggedly pursue their work with the understanding that "the sowing of any idea these days can no longer take place without accepting the need to protect the young seedling, even by violent means." (23) They pay the Cartel in the same coin under the able guidance of the Dentist whose advent radically alters the course of the movement which has hitherto been non-violent and peaceful. The Dentist strictly adheres to his ruthless philosophy of elimination. His bones are said to be filled with "cold rust" in place of marrow. He carries out assassinations with the ease and perfection of an expert surgeon performing an operation. His method is selective. He explains it himself:

> All that we must do is take control of that violence and direct it with a constructive economy. Our people kill but they have this sense of selectiveness . . . select the real kingpins and eliminate them. It is simple, you have to hit the snake on the head to render it harmless. (107)

The Dentist's subversive activities greatly incense the Cartel bosses. In course of time he becomes some kind of a military commander of the Aiyero forces under the charge of Ofeyi who has by now realized that "nothing can be achieved by isolated acts." (100) He busies himself in the mobilization of the progressive elements of society as part of his search for Iriyise and keeps occasionally intellectualizing, while the Dentist plays his tit for tat game with the Cartel. The Dentist has the tacit approval of Ofeyi for his acts. Ofeyi's gradual awareness of the necessity of effectively using violence against violence is implied in the words he speaks to Taiila, the Indian mystic: "I see it, I recognize it. I must confront it." (96)

Ofeyi's search for Iriyise takes him through virtual hell which modern Nigeria is. The search for Iriyise becomes symbolically a voyage of self-discovery for Ofeyi. As an intellectual hitherto he has been most naturally wedded to peaceful means of transforming society. Only of late he has recognized the importance of violence and during this search he finds overwhelming evidence in favour of his changed outlook. The necessity of using violent means assumes added urgency in the wake of the atrocities committed by the Cartel. The various carnages and massacres which Ofeyi witnesses during his search agonize his conscience and place him at the forefront of the Aiyero resistance forces already active under the leadership of his alter-ego the Dentist.

In view of the significance attached to Iriyise and the role she indirectly plays in bringing about a changed outlook in favour of the use of violence in Ofeyi, Soyinka is perhaps justified in devoting almost two-thirds of the novel to her search. This search brings Ofeyi into contact with many dormant progressive forces.

Taking a clue from Zaccheus, the band leader from whose presence Iriyise was forcibly whisked away, Ofeyi wanders from pillar to post with the hope of finding her dead or alive. A complaint at the police station proves futile. Lieutenant Sayi of the Air Force, whose help Ofeyi seeks, advises him to try at the clandestine refugee camps that came up on the outskirts of the city. Contrary to our expectations Sayi is all sympathy for Ofeyi. He and his Air Force men are fiercely opposed to the repressive measures of the army. His help to Ofeyi is generous if not substantial. At the "Tabernacle of Hope," one of the many refugee camps Ofeyi visits, he is hospitably received and guided through the subterranean camp by the kindly catechist Elihu. We also meet here the brave cripple Aliyu, Sergeant-major, food organizer, watchman and general factotum of the camp. Aliyu has saved the church-camp by subjecting himself to the brutality of a stray gang of Cross-river murderers. Ironically Aliyu himself is a Cross-river man. On hearing about the great sacrifice made by Aliyu, Ofeyi gets into a deep introspective mood. The following extract shows him in a deeply disturbed state of mind at the mindless killing of innocent people. He attributes the "blood lust" of the Cross-river rioters to something unusual in the air:

> Ofeyi wondered . . . was the blood lust that seized upon the populace just another legacy of climate? . . . Or was there a truly metaphysical condition called evil, present in epidemic proportions. . . . For this was not a mere question of slaughter. A relish had coloured their actions, a deep hunger of perversion both in inventiveness and magnitude. (270-71)

The brutal and mindless killing of the innocent by the Cross-river men makes Ofeyi cognize the importance of counter-violence more vigorously than before.

On Ahime's advice, Ofeyi visits the mortuary of the government hospital with a flickering hope of finding at least the dead body of Iriyise. The mortuary is packed to capacity with people dying by the hundred everyday. Chalil Ramath, the Indian doctor who is in charge of the hospital, proves to be one of the very significant progressive-minded people that Ofeyi meets during his search. Besides sympathizing with the ideals upheld by Ofeyi the doctor offers him material help at Temoko prison where ultimately Ofeyi sights Iriyise in a state of deep coma. Ofeyi's relation with Ramath's sister Taiila is even deeper. She represents the peace-loving self of Ofeyi. He is so deeply impressed by her calm self-assurance that at least for some moments he vacillates between continuing his search for Iriyise and abandoning it to settle for a peaceful married life with Taiila:

> I, Ofeyi, the eternal intruder, what do I know of these family scenes, these insulated oases of peace, peace. These microcosms of Aiyero. A wild improbable idea rose from within and suffused him—why don't I marry this being and forget the outer chaos. Now, this instant, accept the most tempting interpretation of improbabilities—her presence here, the manipulative sequence of the encounter, accept, accept... no, impose my own need for peace that passeth all misunderstanding. (233)

Ofeyi's essential well disposition towards peace is clear from this musing. He still vacillates occasionally between moods of peace and violence, the first of which he loves and longs for but finds the latter inevitable. It is also possible to give a symbolic dimension of Ofeyi's thoughts here. He has been fighting the malignant forces to restore peace and prosperity to his people. He finds the much longed for peace in Chalil's house and in the presence of Taiila. Perhaps Ofeyi's dream is to extend the mini-peaceful world of Chalil's home to entire Nigeria, even Africa. Viewed in this light, Ofeyi's secret desire to settle down with Taiila does not become escapism but shows his innate love for the prevalence of peace everywhere.

In spite of her professed mysticism, Taiila is one with her brother in supporting Ofeyi and his mission. She in fact accompanies Ofeyi on his visit to the Tabernacle. Ofeyi and Taiila retain their platonic love till the very end.

Crowning upon all these people, representing the progressive forces, comes Suberu, the watch-dog of Temoko prison. He was won over by the evil system quite early in his life. His muscle and mental powers have been badly abused—to subjugate his rebellious fellow victims. Twenty years of servile existence has so hardened his heart that he appears to have no finer feelings at all. Very little of the "human" is left in him. Ofeyi finds himself a prisoner at Temoko and at the mercy of Suberu on the last leg of his search for Iriyise. Ofeyi feels at the moment that only Suberu can rescue him and Iriyise. By his powerful arguments Ofeyi awakens the dormant conscience of Suberu:

> Why can't you see you've been trapped like her [Iriyise] in a capsule of death? The milk rots in the coconut if left too long. . . . The life-yolk rots in the shell if it is not opened in time. (308-9)

Perceiving that the import of his image-laden speech has not gone deep into Suberu's mind, Ofeyi tones down his language and becomes more argumentative:

> Can't I reach you at all Suberu? Can't I reach you in your coffin where you have been forced to lay these twenty years of your short life. . . . Have we all wasted time trying to end the deadly exploitation which traps minds like yours in one lifelong indenture to emptiness? . . . But for faithful dogs like you the Amuris of this world could not trample down humanity with such insolence. You snap at the heels of those who would confront them and afterwards you bury their bones in the back garden. But remember this Suberu . . . only you can sniff out the spot and root out the bones to accuse them. After the licks and caresses, don't complain if the Amuris finally throw you a poisoned bone. (309)

With these words Ofeyi successfully gains the confidence of Suberu though the privileged slave betrays no such signs at the moment. It is a tribute to Ofeyi's persuasive powers to win Suberu to his side. On the symbolical level, the Suberu episode means that Ofeyi has won to his side hundreds and thousands of enslaved Nigerians. There are in his army many Suberus now actively contributing to the progress of the Aiyero ideal.

Meanwhile Dr. Ramath, the Dentist and Zaccheus steal themselves into the prison to help Ofeyi out. To their dismay, they meet with no resistance from Suberu. Carrying the comotose Iriyise away, they had expected Suberu to turn back at the gate but "he stepped outside with them, bolted the gate behind and walked steadfastly ahead." (312) Suberu is no more a slave of Amuri or the Cartel.

Iriyise has been rescued at the end symbolizing the ultimate victory of the intellectual hero and his faithful army of progressive-minded people. All along she has been at the centre of a controversy between Ofeyi and the Dentist who only at the end acknowledges her importance to the furtherance of the Aiyero ideal:

> When the moment arrives a woman like Iriyise become . . . a Chantal, a Deborah, torch and standard-bearer, supermistress of universal insurgence. To abandon such a potential weapon in any struggle is to admit to a lack of foresight. Or imagination. (214)

Iriyise has not died in spite of the great pain inflicted on her by the jackals of the Cartel, so does the Aiyero ideal in spite of the momentary setback it has received. The novel ends on an optimistic note indicating the re ival of Iriyise to life: "Temoko was sealed against the world till dawn. The street emptied at last as the walls and borders shed their last hidden fruit. In the forests, life began to stir." (313)

The Aiyero men have withdrawn their struggle only for the time being, a respite which is perhaps necessary for any ideal to concretize itself. In the words of the Dentist, the exodus of Aiyero people from the Cross-river area means: "The Aiyero ideal treks back to source, but it marks the route for a more determined return." (213) Ofeyi and the Dentist have now withdrawn to their original abode, Aiyero. Ofeyi has seen many progressive elements of society extending their unqualified support to his social mission. Now he is not the lonely intellectual we found at the beginning, struggling to break the fetters of the oppressive system. Now he has got an ideal which has been tested and found effective. He has the support of a faithful army of progressive men who will face the devil if needed. Further, he will no more make scruples of using violence against violence because by now his mind is well-inclined towards the constructive employment of violence. He has in him enthusiasm and a strong will and the backing of men and material. No evil force, however powerful, can deter him from revolutionizing African life on the lines of Aiyero. The sacrifices made by the Aiyero men in Cross-river will lead to the regeneration of life. Season of anomy will be relegated to the pages of history, and peace and harmony will take their rightful place.

By giving a suggestive "cliché" ending to the novel Soyinka has left room for the above hope. In fact, Soyinka has presented the events of the novel in a suggestive manner. Further, with his highly allusive style and elusive method of argument, Soyinka manages to create in us the impression that *Season of Anomy* is not merely a document of some of the undesirable social developments or a blue-print of action plan for the heroic intellectuals of his country. The novel contains many layers of meaning. Soyinka presents in the novel equally important materials and scope to study it from angles other than merely social.

NOTES

1. Eustance Palmer, *The Growth of the African Novel* (London: Heinemann, 1979), pp. 267-68.
2. Olalere Oladitan, "The Nigerian Crisis in the Nigerian Novel," *New West African Literature*; ed. Kolawole Ogungbesan (London:

Heinemann, 1979), p. 14.

3. James Booth, "The Artist and Political Commitment: Wole Soyinka," *Writers and Politics in Nigeria* (London: Hodder and Stoughton, 1981), p. 148
4. Emmanuel Ngara, "Wole Soyinka—Season of anomy," *Stylistic Criticism and African Novel* (London: Heinemann, 1982), p. 115.
5. James Booth, pp. 146-47.
6. Wole Soyinka, *Season of Anomy* (London: Thomas Nelson, 1980), p. 108.
7. Gerald Moore, *Twelve African Writers* (London: Hutchinson Univ. Library for Africa, 1980), p. 229.
8. Eustance Palmer, p. 271.
9. Juliet Okonkwo, "The Essential Unity of Soyinka's *The Interpreters* and *Season of Anomy*," *African Literature Today*, No. 11 (1980), p. 118.
10. Gerald Moore, p..226.
11. Frantz Fanon, *The Wretched of the Earth*, trans. Constance Farrington (Harmondsworth: Penguin, 1982), p. 178.

Towards a Conclusion African Reality and Soyinka's Art in Perspective

In the foregoing chapters, we have discussed the role of African intellectuals in social regeneration through revolution. A study of Soyinka's novels from this angle is likely to give one the impression that he has rather exaggerated notions about the African intellectuals and their effectiveness. This view gains ground from the fact that Soyinka reposes great faith in the infinite possibilities of the intellectuals in his novels, while the reality about most of them is largely at variance with their fictional version. It is generally accepted that the intellectual elite of modern Africa is known for its indulgence in easy going life, taking minimum of risks for fear of jeopardizing their privileged position in society. The confirmation comes from Chinua Achebe, a fellow Nigerian writer: "our intellectuals . . . tend to belong to the same tiny, highly-sought-after group, and to be drawn into the same cycle of time-consuming high life."[1] It can be inferred from Achebe's observation that not many African intellectuals are prepared to sacrifice their "high-life" for the cause of their less fortunate brothers. In fact, quite a few African intellectuals have been either cowed down or won over by the oppressive forces and are, consequently, referred to as "intellect workers."

This is, however, not to suggest that the entire intellectual community of Africa is passive and ineffective. Even among the "intellect workers" there is no dispute about the present order being in need of change for the better. The intellectuals's real nature, characterized by impatience with the establishment, occasionally asserts itself, leading to their falling out of favour with the dictatorial regimes, ruling majority of African states today. There are several instances where dedicated and enlightened people of Africa associated themselves with various struggles against oppression in the face of grave threat to their personal safety. The important Anglophone writers of Africa namely, Ayi Kwei Armah, Ngugi wa Thiong'o and Soyinka himself were forced to go into exile because of their active participation in popular movements. The contribution of Victor Banjo, a leader of Soyinka's "Third Force," to the awakening of Nigerians to the truth behind the Biafran war is well known. The young Nigerian poet Christopher Okigbo sacrificed even his life for the Biafran cause.

Viewed in this light, Soyinka's novels cannot be dismissed as figments of his elitist imagination. In these novels, he evinced great faith in the ability of the intellectuals to lead society and rightly so. If some intellectuals have grudgingly joined hands with the repressive forces, they are isolated exceptions. Majority of them are not indifferent to the problems of their fellow men. At least a small section of them has openly come out against all types of corrupt institutions in recent times. The fact that these intellectuals are active in public life is exemplified by the ouster of the notorious Ugandan dictator Idi Amin, against whom the intellectuals of Africa built a strong public opinion. The recent release of Nelson Mandela from prison and the establishment of the SWAPO Government under the leadership of Sam Nujoma in Namibia at the end of a long period of colonial rule while validating Soyinka's belief in the viability of the leadership of the African intellectuals mark a significant triumph for them in both moral and actual terms.

The writer's task becomes all the more difficult if he is to depict the African reality discussed above. A mechanical portrayal of this reality may render a work of art journalistic. So Soyinka calls into play all his creative abilities to maintain a poise between realism and art. A thorough analysis of his novels inevitably leads one to this conclusion.

Soyinka's realism is in direct contrast with that of Ngugi and Achebe. In his zealous commitment to social cause Ngugi appears to have overlooked the artistic validity of his work. His ideological bias has made him frankly didactic. Some of the passages in his novels read almost like political pejorations aimed at brainwashing the audience and goading them into immediate action. But such open statement is not agreeable to Soyinka. He does not sacrifice artistic values even when dealing with political and social issues. Further, unlike Ngugi, Soyinka has never attempted a clinical dissection of his society nor has he claimed that his understanding of the society is complete. "On the other hand," says James Booth, "he is constantly examining his experience, attempting to understand himself and his society: to find a constructive role. And in this endeavour perhaps more of value emerges than from, say, the rather wooden, text-book demonstrations of neo-colonial forces to be found in such novels as Ngugi's ideologically pure *Petals of Blood.*"[2]

In conformity with his much-publicized opinion: "Art for art's sake is just another piece of deodorized dog-shit,"[3] Achebe has assigned the novelist the role of a teacher. In his commitment to the exposure of society, Achebe has over-simplified the Nigerian reality, especially in his later novels. In contrast, by not committing to any narrow philosophy or dogma, Soyinka has retained the artistic freedom which makes a writer primarily what he is. The basic difference between the social approaches of Achebe and Soyinka is vividly shown by James Booth: "Where Achebe's meticulous and lucid analyses plot the impact of social and political influences upon the individual, Soyinka conveys the tangled density of individual experience, the texture of life in process."[4]

Whatever may be the form, realism has been an essential element in the works of all the African writers. They have been necessitated by history to fictionally relive the African reality because they are placed in a complex socio-political and cultural situation in which they cannot shirk their responsibility as pathfinders for the future. They have been shouldering this responsibility in their different ways, subject to their limitations. But in this process what testifies to the artistic calibre of these writers is the delicate balance which they maintain between their social and artistic commitments. Soyinka consciously maintains this balance between the not so harmonious demands and that is where perhaps he has an edge over other writers.

Soyinka's artistic commitment merits an elaborate treatment. Soyinka dearly upholds artistic values in his novels even at the cost of being misunderstood or even not understood by many. In order to enhance the artistic value of his work, Soyinka adapts a complex style which sometimes renders him vulnerable to the charge of elitism. The complexity of Soyinka's style has intrigued the Nigerian critics such as O.O. Enekwe and Theo Vincent so much that they have gone so far as to question the very social relevance of his work. The reader should transcend the hurdles posed by style and should be on the same wave-length as Soyinka, and highly sensitive besides, to appreciate the real worth of Soyinka's fiction. Soyinka has invested his style with great richness which sometimes borders on obscurity. He is vehemently opposed to toning down his language and style to the ordinary reader's assimilative capacity. James Booth was so provoked by the "obscurity" of Soyinka as to say "like the European modernist he [Soyinka] often resorts to a deliberate obscurity, designed to make his art the exclusive preserve of the initiates."[5] But the charge of obscurity does not seem to have worried Soyinka as is clear from his words: "everybody obtains from a work of art very many different things at many different levels and one should never worry unduly that a certain section of one's . . . readership is not appreciating it."[6]

The complexity of Soyinka's style results from his use of language, myth, symbolism and allegory that have been closely and profitably interwoven into the texture of his two novels. Much of Soyinka's celebrated obscurity is a direct result of the handling of the English tongue. He is fond of archaic words and loves to coin new words and phrases. Something of the dramatist and something of the poet, both of which Soyinka is, always find their way into his novels. Following is one of the many passages from *Season of Anomy* that could be cited as an example of Soyinka's dramatic rendering of dialogue and the poetic quality of the language:

> He laughed, self-deprecatingly. "Don't look for lines of the tragic romance of life on my face."

> Crestfallen, she looked away. "I don't mean. . . ."
>
> Gently, he took her hand. "Neither did I. All I meant was . . . I have been too busy or too wholesomely dissatisfied to be unhappy."
>
> "Ah yes . . . your eternal discontent. . . ."
>
> "Divine. What's happened since? It used to be divine discontent."
>
> She shook her head. "I don't believe that any longer. It threatens to last a lifetime if life is what I observe . . . what I have observed since I came here. What I still see in you. Nothing that eats the human life away has the smallest touch of divinity. It is all so . . . insignificant, I mean, ultimately. Well isn't it?"[7]

Unfortunately, Soyinka has not successfully transposed his talent to the narrative mode so far. But Emmanuel Ngara appears to feel that Soyinka's dramatic language in the novels is deliberately used and is aimed at evoking "a sense of horror . . . of pity in the reader, pity for suffering humanity."[8]

Another quality peculiar to Soyinka's style is the structural use of myth. Myths run in close parallel with the main narrative of his novels. Some of the characters too have mythological dimensions. The mythical frame of *Season of Anomy* and the mythical significance of Egbo are easily perceivable. The Orpheus-Eurydice myth runs parallel with the Ofeyi-Iriyise relationship. In Kola's Pantheon, Egbo has been represented as Ogun, the Yoruba god of creativity and destruction. Kola appears to have rightly done so because Egbo has been a constant source of inspiration to the other interpreters which is in one sense something creative in him and there is also always something destructive about what Egbo does. By failing to make an early choice in life he has deprived the Osa subjects of the opportunity of being ruled by an enlightened chief. By deflowering the innocent college student at his groove resort, he has permanently marred her future prospects.

Soyinka has profitably used symbolism, if not so extensively as D.H. Lawrence. Some of his characters reveal symbolic dimensions at one stage or the other. Iriyise, who has been realistically portrayed until her abduction by the Cartel men, suddenly turns symbolic to personify the Aiyero ideal. The titles chosen by Soyinka for different chapters of the *Season of Anomy* namely, Seminal, Buds, Tentacles, Harvest and Spores are suggestive of rebirth symbolism. They symbolize the sowing of Aiyero ideal in the Cross-river area, its spread and the partial success it meets with.

Thus Soyinka's style contributes to the total beauty and effect of his novels. If *Season of Anomy* ends on a subdued note suggesting that the intellectual hero will ultimately emerge triumphant in restoring meaning to African life and peace and security to society, it is because Soyinka believes in understatement. Viewed from this angle, it can be argued that Soyinka's complex style has more value to the discerning reader than that of those writers who simplify their language in order to reach a larger readership. Emphasizing the importance of complex style, Soyinka himself says that "the energy and passion of social revolution appears . . . to quarry into the metaphorical resources of language in order to brand its message deeper in the heart of humanity."[9]

In the light of the above discussion the obscurity of Soyinka becomes part of a greater purpose and not just an effort on his part to ignore the ordinary reader. The ideological and mythical dimensions of Soyinka's works, the minute analysis of society and deep insights into the African psyche and his exploitation of the resourcefulness of the English language lend his works variety and depth besides earning them universal acceptability and acclaim. In the process, Soyinka emerges an African novelist of unique distinction.

NOTES

1. Chinua Achebe, "What do the African Intellectuals Read?" *Morning Yet on Creation Day* (London: Heinemann, 1975), p. 38.
2. James Booth, "The Artist and Political Commitment: Wole Soyinka," *Writers and Politics in Nigeria* (London: Hodder and

Stoughton, 1981), pp. 123-24.
3. Chinua Achebe, "Africa and her Writers," *Morning Yet on Creation Day*, p. 18.
4. James Booth, p. 132.
5. *Ibid.*, p. 119.
6. Mary David, "The Maverick: An Interview with Soyinka," *The Illustrated Weekly of India*, 9-15 Nov. 1986, p. 38.
7. Wole Soyinka, *Season of Anomy* (London: Thomas Nelson, 1980), p. 237.
8. Emmanuel Ngara, "Wole Soyinka—*Season of Anomy*," *Stylistic Criticism and African Novel* (London: Heinemann, 1982), p. 110.
9. Wole Soyinka, *Myth, Literature and the African World* (London: Cambridge Univ. Press, 1976), p. 63.

Bibliography

PRIMARY SOURCES

A. *Books*

NOVELS

The Interpreters. London: Heinemann, 1970.
Season of Anomy. London: Thomas Nelson, 1980.

PLAYS

The Swamp Dwellers. Oxford: Oxford Univ. Press, 1964.
A Dance of the Forests. Oxford: Oxford Univ. Press, 1963.
The Strong Breed. Oxford: Oxford Univ. Press, 1964.
The Road. Oxford: Oxford Univ. Press, 1965.
The Bacchae of Euripides. Oxford: Oxford Univ. Press, 1973.
The Lion and the Jewel. Oxford: Oxford Univ. Press, 1963.
Madmen and Specialists. London: Metheun, 1971.
A Play of Giants. London: Metheun, 1984.
Kongi's Harvest. Oxford: Oxford Univ. Press, 1967.
The Trials of Brother Jero. Oxford: Oxford Univ. Press, 1964.
Jero's Metamorphosis. London: Metheun, 1973.

POETRY

A Shuttle in the Crypt. London: Rex Collings, 1972.
Idanre and Other Poems. London: Metheun, 1967.

NON-FICTION

The Man Died. London: Rex Collings, 1972.
Ake: The Years of Childhood. London: Rex Collings.

CRITICISM

Myth, Literature and the African World. London: Cambridge University Press, 1976.

B. *ARTICLES*

"Cross-Currents: The 'New African' After Cultural Encounters." *Writers in East-West Encounter: New Cultural Bearings,* ed. Guy Amirthanayagam. London: Macmillan, 1982. Pp. 51-63.
"The Writers in a Modern African State." *The Writer in Modern Africa,* ed. Per Wastberg. Uppsala: Scandinavian Institute of Africa Studies, 1968.
"Electoral Fraud and the Western Press." *South Africa Outlook* (Jan. 1984), pp. 7-9.
"This Past Must Address its Present." *Mainstream,* No.16, 3 Jan. 1987, pp. 15-22.
"We Africans Must Speak One Tongue." *Africa,* XX, 9 (1979), pp. 22-23.
"Salutations to the Gut." *Reflections³Nigerian Prose and Verse,* ed. Frances Ademola. Lagos: African University Press, 1962. Pp. 117-123.

SECONDARY SOURCES

A. *BOOKS*

Achebe, Chinua. *Things Fall Apart.* London: Heinemann, 1958.
------. *Arrow of God.* New York: Doubleday, 1969.
------. *No Longer At Ease.* London: Heinemann, 1975.

------. *Morning Yet on Creation Day*. London: Heinemann, 1975.
Armah, Ayi Kwei. *The Beautiful Ones Are Not Yet Born*. Beirut: York Press, 1982.
------. *Two Thousand Seasons*. London: Heinemann, 1979.
Booth, James. "The Artist and Political Commitment: Wole Soyinka." *Writers and Politics in Nigeria*. London: Hodder and Stoughton, 1981. Pp. 114-65.
Fanon, Frantz. *The Wretched of the Earth*. Harmondsworth: Penguin, 1982.
Jones, Eldred Durosimi. *The Writing of Wole Soyinka*. London: Heinemann, 1973.
Larson, Charles R. *The Emergence of African Fiction*. Hong Kong: Macmillan, 1971.
Lawson, William. *The Western Scar: The Theme of the Been-to in West African Fiction*. Ohio: Ohio University Press, 1982.
Moore, Gerald. "Across the Primeval Gulf." *Twelve African Writers*. London: Hutchinson, 1980. Pp. 218-35.
------. *Wole Soyinka*. London: Evan Brothers, 1971.
Ngara, Emmanuel. "Wole Soyinka's *Season of Anomy*." *Stylistic Criticism and the African Novel*. London: Heinemann, 1982. Pp. 99-116.
Palmer, Eustance. "Wole Soyinka." *The Growth of the African Novel*. London: Heinemann, 1979. Pp. 240-87.
Thiong'o, Ngugi wa. *Home Coming*. New York: Lawrence Hill, 1973.

B. *ARTICLES*

Ackley, D. "Wole Soyinka's *The Interpreters*." *Black Orpheus*, II (1971), pp. 54-67.
Allen, S. "Two Writers: Senghor and Soyinka." *Negro Digest* (June 1967), pp. 54-67
Amuta, Chidi. "Nigerian Civil War and the Evolution of Nigerian Fiction." *Canadian Journal of African Stuies*, XVII, 1 (1983), pp. 85-99
------. "Criticism, Ideology and Society: the Instance of Nigerian

Literature." *UFAHAMU*, XII, 2 (1983), pp. 116-38.

-------. Ideology and Form in the Contemporary Nigerian Novel." *Commonwealth: Essays and Studies*, VII, 1 (1984), pp. 94-105.

Attwell, David. "Wole Soyinka's *The Interpreters:* Suggestions on Context and History." *English in Africa*, VII, 1, "n.d." 59-71.

Balogun, F.O. "Evolution of the African Literary Hero (The Hero as a Mirror of Aesthetics)." *Nigeria Magazine*, CXLVI (1983), pp. 51-61.

Baran, Paul, "The Commitment of the Intellectual." *Intellectual and the 'Left' in Africa*, No. 32 (April 1985), p. 47.

Brown, David Maugham. "Interpreting and *The Interpreters:* Wole Soyinka and Practical Criticism." *English in Africa*, VI, 2 (1979), pp. 51-62.

Chinweizu. "Soyinka's Neo-Tarzanism: A Reply." *Okike*, XIV (1978), pp. 43-51.

Conlon, Virginia. "Emerging National Literature in Nigeria." *South African Outlook* (May 1984), pp. 72-75.

Crow, Brian and Oga S Abah. "Soyinka and the Voice of Vision." *The Journal of Commonwealth Literature*, XVII, 1 (1982), pp. 100-22.

d'Almeida, Irene Assiba. "From Social Commitment to Ideological Awareness: A Study of Soyinka's *The Interpreters* and *Season of Anomy*." *UFAHAMU*, X, 3 (Spring 1981), pp. 13-28.

Ezigbo, Emeka Okeke. "The Role of the Nigerian Writer in a Carthaginian Society." *Okike*, XXI (1982), pp. 28-37.

Feuser, Willfried. "Nigerian Civil War in Fiction." *New Literature Review*, XI (Nov. 1982), pp. 6-20.

Galie, Etienne. "The European and African Critical Reception of Wole Soyinka." *AFRAM News Letter*, XV (1982), pp. 12-22.

Gerald, Albert S. "Literary Tradition and Literary Change in Black Africa." *The Journal of Commonwealth Literature*, XIX, 1 (1984), pp. 44-50.

Gibbs, James, "Interpreting *The Interpreters*." *Joliso*, I, 2 (1973), pp. 110-26.

Green, Robert. "African Literary Criticism: The Banality of Cannibalism." *The Journal of Commonwealth Literature*, XIX, 1 (1984), pp. 52-63.

Gurnah, A.R. "*The Interpreters:* Technique as Structure." *Ariel*, XII, 2 (1982), pp. 67-81.

Houbein, Lolo. "*The Interpreters:* Wole Soyinka." *ACLALS Bulletin*, V, 3 (1980), pp. 98-111.

Izevbaye, D.S. "Time in the African Novel." *The Journal of Commonwealth Literature*, XVII, 1 (1982), pp. 74-86.

Johnson, Joyce. "The Traditional Gulf: A Discussion of Wole Soyinka's *Season of Anomy*." *World Literature Written in English*, XVIII (1979), pp. 287-301. Hereafter cited as *WLWE*.

Jones, Eldred. "Wole Soyinka's *The Interpreters:* Reading Notes." *African Literature Today*, II, "n.d," pp. 42-60.

------. "Interpreting *The Interpreters*." *The Bulletin of the Association for African Literature in English*, No. 4, pp. 13-18.

July, Robert. "The Artist's Credo: The Political Philosophy of Wole Soyinka." *Journal of Modern African Studies*, XIX, 3, "n.d," pp. 477-98.

Kiiru, M. "Elitism in Soyinka's *The Interpreters*." *Basura*, VI, I (1974), pp. 12-16.

King, Bruce. "*The Interpreters* by Wole Soyinka." *Black Orpheus*, XIX (1966), p. 55.

Lodge, Tom. "Nigerian Literature and the Civil War." *Work in Progress*, V (1978), pp. 21-58.

Maduakor, Obi. "Soyinka's *Season of Anomy:* Ofeyi's Quest." *International Fiction Review*, VII (1980), pp. 85-89.

Mallikarjuna Rao, P. "No Longer At Ease: A Note on the African Writing." *Kakatiya Journal of English Studies*, VII (1985-86), pp. 73-81.

Moore, Gerald. "The First Novel." *The New African*, IV, 7 (1965), p. 156.

Nandan, Satendra. "Beyond Colonialism: the Artist as Healer." In

South Pacific Images, ed Chris Tiffin So. Queensland: Pacific Association for Commonwealth Literature, 1978. Pp. 11-25.

Nuolim, Charles. "The Nigerian Tradition in the Novel." *Commonwealth Novel in English*, II, 2 (1983), pp. 22-40.

Nwoga, D. "*The Interpreters* by Wole Soyinka." *Ibadan*, XXII (1966), pp. 62-63.

Obiechina, E.N. "Perception of Colonialism in West African Literature." In *Literature and Modern West African Culture*, ed. D.I. Nwoga. Benin City: Ethiope Publications, 1978. Pp. 51-60.

Ogungbesan, Kolawole. "Wole Soyinka and the Novelist's Responsibility in Africa." In *New West African Literature*, ed. Kolawole Ogungbesan. London: Heinemann, 1979. Pp. 1-8.

Okonkwo, Juliet. "Intellectual as Political Activist: A Character Type in Recent African Fiction." *Africaine*, CXXX (1984), pp. 71-92.

------. "The Essential Unity of Soyinka's *The Interpreters* and *Season of Anomy*." *African Literature Today*, XI (1980), pp. 110-21.

Oladitan, Olalere. "The Nigerian Crisis in the Nigerian Novel." *New West African Literature*, ed. Kolawole Ogungbesan. London: Heinemann, 1979. Pp. 10-20.

Osundare, Niyi. "Words of Iron, Sentences of Thunder: Aspects of Soyinka's Prose Style." *African Literature Today*, XIII (1983), pp. 24-37.

Palmer, Eustance. "Wole Soyinka's *Season of Anomy*." *WLWE*, XVII (1978), pp. 435-49.

Pearse, Adetokunbo. "Symbolic Characterization of Women in the Plays and Prose of Wole Soyinka." *Ba Shiru*, IV, 1/2 (1978), pp. 39-46.

Pollard, Phyllis. "Myth, Literature and Ideology: A Reading of Wole Soyinka's *Season of Anomy*." *The Journal of Commonwealth Literature*, XIX (1984), pp. 74-85.

Ravenscraft, Arthur. "African Literature V: Novels of Disillusion." *The Journal of Commonwealth Literature*, VI

(Jan. 1969), pp. 120-37.

Riemenschneider, Dieter. "Biafran War in Nigerian Literature." *The Journal of Commonwealth Literature*, XVIII, 1 (1983), pp. 55-68.

Webb, Hugh. "Soyinka's Novelistic Autobiography." *New Literature Review*, V (1978), pp. 11-21.

Wilkinson, Nick. "Literary Incomprehension: Wole Soyinka's Own Way with a Mode." *Nsukka Studies in African Literature*, I, 1 (1978), pp. 44-53.

Wright, Edgar. "Wole Soyinka's *Season of Anomy.*" *African Literature Today*, VIII (1976), pp. 115-20.

C. *INTERVIEWS*

David, Mary. "The Maverick." An interview with Wole Soyinka, *The Illustrated Weekly of India*, 9-15 Nov. 1986, p. 57.

Dyson, Soyini. "Interviews Wole Soyinka." *Black Books Bulletin*, VII, 1 (1980), pp. 36-39, 47.

Jeyifo, Biodun. "Soyinka at 50." *West Africa*, 27 August 1984, pp. 1729-31.

Nkosi, et al. *African Writers Talking*, ed. Dennis Duerden and Cosmo Pieterse. London: Heinemann, 1972. Pp.169-80.

Thiong'o, Ngugi Wa. "The Commitment of the Intellectual." In interview with Obi Bini, *Intellectual and the "Left" in Africa*, No. 32 (April, 1985), p. 19.

Index

Achebe, Chinua 23, 25, 29, 36n, 80, 81, 82, 85n, 86n
A Man of the People 25
Armah, Ayi Kwei 25, 29, 81
Arrow of God 29

Beautiful Ones Are Not Yet Born, The 25

Eurydice 72, 84

Fanon, Frantz 22-23, 28, 29, 30, 31, 35, 35n, 36n, 49, 53, 54, 56n, 59, 70, 79n
Freud, Sigmund 30

Hegel 22
Home Coming 35n, 56n
Hume 22

Idanre 29
Interpreters, The 26, 27, 30, 32, 33, 34, 35, 36n, **37-56**, 56n, 59, 60, 64, 79n

Lawrence, D.H. 30, 84
Lion and the Jewel, The 27
Locke 22

Madmen and Specialists 27
Man Died, The 58
Montesquieu 22
Morning Yet on Creation Day 36n, 85n, 86n

Ngara, Emmanuel 59, 79n, 84, 86n

Okigbo, Christopher 81
Orpheus 72, 84

Petals of Blood 82

Road, The 27-28, 46

Season of Anomy 27, 29, 30, 31, 32, 33, 34, 35, 36n, 54, **57-79**, 79n, 83, 84, 85, 86n
Sembene, Ousmane 66
Sons and Lovers 30
Swift, Jonathan 52

Things Fall Apart 29
Thiong'o, Ngugi Wa 25, 29, 35n, 36n, 55, 56n, 66, 81, 82
Trials of Brother Jero 46
Two Thousand Seasons 29

Voltaire 22

Wretched of the Earth, The 28, 35n, 56n, 79n